Football
Grounds

THEN & NOW

MICHAEL HEATLEY AND DANIEL FORD

DIAL PRESS

First published 1994

ISBN 07110 2302 6

© Michael Heatley 1994

Published by Dial Press

an imprint of Ian Allan Ltd, Terminal House, Station Approach, Shepperton, Surrey TW17 8AS. Printed by Ian Allan Printing Ltd, Coombelands House, Coombelands Lane, Addlestone, Weybridge, Surrey KT15 1HY.

PICTURE CREDITS

Aerofilms:
9T, 10, 11T, 13B, 14-15, 16, 17T, 18-19, 20B, 29T, 30T, 33B, 34-35, 37T, 38T, 38M, 39R, 40T, 41T, 42T, 42B, 43, 46B, 47BL, 50, 51BL, 52B, 54, 57B, 58B, 58T, 61, 62T, 64, 65T, 66T, 67T, 67M, 78T, 81B, 89T, 90T, 92T, 96T, 98T, 100T, 101B, 104B, 106T, 108M, 109T, 110B, 112, 114-115, 117, 119B, 121B, 124T, 126T, 127B, 128T, 136R, 142T, 148B, 149T, 150B, 152T, 153, 153B

Colorsport:
8, 9B, 11B, 21T, 22, 23, 24, 25, 28T, 29B, 30M, 32, 36T, 40B, 45B, 51T, 51BR, 53B, 55M, 55B, 56B, 63, 66B, 69T, 72, 80, 82B, 84, 86TIns, 90B, 91, 92B, 94B, 96B, 98B, 100B, 101T, 102T, 102B, 103B, 104T, 106B, 111T, 111B, 113B, 114T, 116T, 18T, 120T, 122B, 123I, 129T, 130R, 132T, 134T, 134B, 135B, 136L, 138T, 139B, 141B, 142B, 143, 148T, 149B, 150T, 151M, 152B

Ken Coton:
6T, 6B, 7B, 24T, 31B, 34L, 42M, 44B, 46T, 49B, 65B, 67B, 69B, 74T, 78B, 83B, 85B, 88T, 93M, 95B, 105T, 107B, 115B, 118B, 119T, 125T, 129B, 133B

EMPics:
5T, 5B, 12, 13T, 14, 17B, 18, 19Ins, 26, 28B, 30B, 31T, 33T, 35B, 37B, 38B, 39L, 41B, 45T, 47T, 47BR, 48, 49T, 55T, 57T, 60T, 69M, 70, 71T, 73BL, 73BR, 74-75, 79, 82T, 83T, 85T, 86-87, 88B, 89B, 93B, 94T, 95T, 96TL, 99B, 103T, 105B, 107T, 110T, 113T, 113M, 116B, 121T, 122T, 123, 124B, 125B, 126B, 129M, 131Ins, 132M, 135T, 136R, 137Ins, 138B, 139T, 140T, 141T, 151B

Peter Bishop:
130L

Crystal Palace:
FC: 52T, 53T

Everton FC:
56T

Glasgow Rangers:
FC: 151T

Leicester City:
FC: 68

Lincoln City FC:
71M, 71B

Liverpool FC:
73T

Lobb Partnership:
20T, 21B, 62B, 155, 156T, 156B, 157B, 158, 158-159, 160

Peter Mason:
120B

McAlpine/S Arnold:
154-155

Middlesbrough FC:
157T

Mowlem Construction:
44T, 128B

Norwich City FC:
93T

Nottingham Forest FC:
97T

RJS Programmes:
60B

Scunthorpe United FC:
109M

Mark Shanahan:
99T

John Staff:
108T, 108B, 109B

Swindon Town FC:
122T

Tranmere Rovers FC:
131T

Dennis Turner Collection:
59

Walsall FC:
132B

Watford FC:
4T, 133T

Wolverhampton Wanderers FC:
7T, 140-141

CONTENTS

ACKNOWLEDGEMENTS

This book has been a team effort in which, although my name is on the cover, I have played only a part. Daniel Ford contributed the Introduction and Future Grounds sections, as well as writing many of the club entries: Graham Betts also made numerous contributions on the club front. Ian Welch oversaw the progress of the book through the production stages, and Simon Joslin designed it. Finally, thanks are due to Dennis Turner for his proof reading and corrections.

All the above-named are involved in the writing, production or design of *Matchday*, the official magazine of the Endsleigh League which, since the book was written, has been taken over by Ian Allan Publishing.

Michael Heatley

Thanks to:

Derek Wilson at Lobb Partnership, especially for assistance with the Future Grounds section; AD Rowing, Chief Executive Scunthorpe United FC; Jimmy Frizzell, General Manager Manchester City FC; FD Corfe, Chief Executive Tranmere Rovers FC; John Goldsmith, Director Leyton Orient FC; Simon Arnold, for information on the Severnside Development at Bristol; Mike and Paula Hinson.

Clubs who kindly returned our questionnaires:

Arsenal, Aston Villa, Birmingham City, Blackburn Rovers, Brentford, Bristol Rovers, Burnley, Cardiff City, Charlton Athletic, Chelsea, Chester City, Coventry City, Crystal Palace, Exeter City, Fulham, Grimsby Town, Huddersfield Town, Ipswich Town, Leeds United, Leicester City, Leyton Orient, Manchester City, Manchester United, Middlesbrough, Millwall, Newcastle United, Northampton Town, Norwich City, Nottingham Forest, Oldham Athletic, Oxford United, Plymouth Argyle, Preston North End, Queens Park Rangers, Reading, Scunthorpe United, Sheffield Wednesday, Southampton, Southend United, Stoke City, Sunderland, Swindon Town, Tottenham Hotspur, Tranmere Rovers, Walsall, Watford, West Bromwich Albion, Wimbledon, Wolverhampton Wanderers, Wrexham, Wycombe Wanderers, Aberdeen, Celtic, Hibernian, Rangers.

Dedicated to Tony 'Chugger' Ford

Introduction

Football stadia in Britain have undergone more changes in the last few years than at any other time in the previous century. Meeting the sheer scale (and cost) of the carrying out of the measures imposed on football clubs by the Taylor Report in 1990 at one time seemed an impossible task. For many clubs, sadly, it still is. But for those who have carried out the work set out in the Report (most notably, that terraces are removed from any ground hosting Premiership or First Division football) the results are impressive. The Taylor Inquiry, which was set in motion following the deaths of 95 fans at Hillsborough on 17 April 1989, has undoubtedly changed the face of football grounds throughout Britain.

For years grounds in this country were berated when compared to the stadia of Europe and America. Now, despite the refusal of clubs to pool resources and share facilities, as Justice Taylor suggested, we again have stadia of which to be proud. The decision to stage the expanded European Championship Finals in England in 1996 (16 countries will participate instead of the previous eight) is the ultimate accolade for the authorities which finally, after the tragedy at Hillsborough, demanded that grounds were brought into the modern age. The eight grounds which will be used are Anfield, Elland Road, Hillsborough, Old Trafford, St James' Park, the City Ground, Villa Park and Wembley.

European and South American grounds are revered for their size and splendour; but for the British fan the ground has always been more than simply a place to watch a game of football. It is the heart of the club itself. That is why, despite the obvious financial advantages, few supporters will accept their turf being tainted by groundsharing (clubs often take their nicknames from the ground).

It is striking, nevertheless, just how many clubs, especially during World War 2, have successfully shared grounds, most often with their neighbours and rivals.

One of the biggest effects of the recent developments is that capacities have tumbled. In the club sections, note the huge differences between the capacity recorded in 1971 and those of today. Highest attendance figures (many of which remain from the 1930s boom years) have also been included and these too give a fascinating insight into the shrinking capacities of our nation's football grounds.

Above: Watford's futuristic Vicarage Road development takes shape.

Below: The Ibrox tragedy of 1902 – an early warning of the dangers of terracing.

The spaces on the terraces have been replaced by a range of facilities and activities which would astonish the sport's early supporters. Executive boxes, in which business clients can be wined and dined, have generated valuable income for clubs despite criticism from the 'ordinary' spectator. Incorporating shops, offices and extra sporting facilities for community use into many of the grounds' redevelopment plans is also crucial for the survival of many clubs.

Football has realised for a long time that it could not exist from gate money alone. A survey by the Royal Town Planning Institute in 1993 found that as many as 54 clubs have considered commercial redevelopment to assist in

the funding of ground improvements. The same source suggests that 63 clubs have considered long-term relocation during the last five years. At the time of writing, those clubs actively seeking a new home number 24.

Of the clubs who have already packed their bags Scunthorpe settled at Glanford Park in 1988, while Walsall and Chester moved in 1990 and 1992 respectively. More recently Millwall transferred their headquarters some 400yd to a 20,000-seater stadium at Bermondsey in 1993, and a year later Huddersfield said farewell to their famous Leeds Road ground to take up residence at the futuristic, multi-purpose Kirklees Stadium.

Above: The barriers came down after Hillsborough, permitting this good natured pitch invasion at Ninian Park in 1993.

Below: Keeping the pitch playable in wintry condition remains a problem. Aston Villa used a plastic covering.

SAFETY AT FOOTBALL GROUNDS
Football grounds have hardly been strangers to tragedy. In 1902, 26 people died and over 500 were injured when terracing collapsed at Ibrox during an international between England and Scotland. Another fan lost his life in a crush at Burnley in 1924 and some 22 years later 33 people died and 400 were injured at Bolton. Ibrox was the scene of two further deaths in 1957 when a wooden barrier collapsed on a stairway leading off the terraces. Tragically it was on this same stairway that 66 fans were crushed to death in 1971 after a Rangers v Celtic game. Again, the barriers (made of steel) had given way.

However, it was a series of tragic events in the 1980s that forced the authorities to completely rethink safety at sporting events. On 11 May 1985 a fire engulfed a wooden stand at Valley Parade, home of Bradford City, killing 56 spectators and injuring many others. On the same day, a young boy was killed and 200 others injured when a wall collapsed at St Andrews, Birmingham, following rioting from Leeds fans. Two weeks later a similar incident killed 39 fans at the Heysel Stadium in Brussels before the European Cup Final between Liverpool and Juventus. Then, on 17 April 1989, in the biggest ever tragedy at a football ground in this country, 95 fans died in a crush at Hillsborough. That same decade deaths occurred at football grounds in Ibague, Colombia; Moscow, Russia; Cali, Colombia; Tripoli, Libya; Kathmandu, Nepal and Lagos, Nigeria.

The authorities had to act. They did – first with the Popplewell Report in 1986 and four years later with the Taylor Report, which eventually became law as the Football Spectators Act. Both have had a profound effect on the shaping of football grounds in Britain.

Prior to the 1980s, safety at sporting events was covered by the Safety of Sports Grounds Act 1975. Clubs which had a ground with a capacity exceeding 10,000 had to obtain a safety certificate from their local authorities. After the initial inspection, clubs were given a number of months (varied depending on the authority and the circumstances) to implement any measures laid down by the inspector. Any sections of the ground which could not be brought up to scratch had to be closed. For economic reasons the Act was applied only to clubs playing in the (then) First Division and Scottish Premier, although English Second Division grounds were later brought under its control. Thus, clubs playing in the two lower divisions, regardless of the size of their ground, did not have to obtain a certificate.

The Popplewell Report was published in January 1986, following the Bradford fire and riot at Birmingham. Justice Popplewell recommended that safety certificates should be renewed annually

and should also apply to grounds holding other sporting events. Inflammable materials, such as wood, were not to be used in the building of any new structures and smoking was to be banned from any older stands which continued to be used.

Also, while recognising some limited benefit in the national membership scheme for football supporters proposed by the government at the time, Popplewell expressed concern at the practical difficulties in setting up such a scheme. He also suggested a full review of the sale of alcohol within grounds.

Finally — and most significantly, as events at Hillsborough three years later were to prove — the Report called for the implementation of well-designed perimeter fencing, with plenty of exits.

The Taylor Report, following the tragedy at Sheffield, was published on 29 January 1990. It was fiercely critical of safety and conditions at football grounds and proposed a major, if not revolutionary, change. The main thrust of the Report was that all terracing should be removed and stadia made all-seater. First and Second Division clubs were given until August 1994 to comply, with the deadline for the Third and Fourth Divisions five years later. Aberdeen had been all-seater since 1978 and Coventry experimented with the idea in the early 1980s, but the mere idea of every club becoming all-seater sent shock waves through football. Initial estimates put the overall cost at £295 million.

In total there were 76 recommendations in the Taylor Report, which included:

- Abandoning the government's national ID scheme.
- Removing spikes from fences and limiting them in height to 2.2 metres.
- Outlawing ticket touting, pitch invasions, obscene and racist abuse.
  (The Criminal Justice and Public Order Bill was amended in April 1994 to make it illegal to sell tickets at more than face value. Police were given the power to confiscate tickets and touts now run the risk of a maximum £5,000 fine or six months' imprisonment.)
- Improving medical and first aid facilities with doctors available at or near to every ground.
- Reducing the speed at which spectators pass through the turnstiles from 750 per hour to 660 per hour.
- Better training for police and stewards on crowd control.

The Report condemned the clubs for their 'chilling complacency' and accused management of being more concerned with 'boardroom power struggles and wheeler dealing' than with the fans. It called for new thinking by everyone. 'The years of patching up grounds, of having periodic disasters and narrowly avoiding many others by muddling through on a wing and a prayer, must be over' the Report stated.

Southampton were one of the first clubs to outline the practical difficulties of survival following the publication of the Report. Club secretary Brian Truscott said: 'We could never convert the Dell to all-seater and maintain an adequate capacity level in the long term.'

The government immediately stated that there would be no

Above: Arrival at Eastville in 1971. Bristol Rovers' former ground is no longer used for League football.

Below left: Crowd control is not a new problem, as these fans at Millwall's Den prove in 1972.

public money available for the redevelopment of football grounds, a view *The Times* backed in an editorial: 'The government's concern is with public safety and public order. Public opinion will support it in believing that football must now put its own house in order at its own expense.' Meanwhile, many clubs made it clear that they did not have the funds necessary to implement all the changes asked of them.

The government demanded change and the football clubs agreed — but neither wanted to fund the change. Thankfully for the sport, and probably for the very survival of many football clubs, this hard line softened. A compromise was eventually reached when the government announced it was to reduce the levy on the football pools from 42.5% to 40% — the difference going to the Football Trust, who would administer the fund to help clubs with their ground developments. It was a measure called for by Ernie Clay, then Fulham chairman, after the Bradford fire.

In August 1993 the government announced a five-year extension to the reduction in pools duty, releasing a further £100 million for Second and Third Division clubs. It was reported that grants of £86 million had generated building work worth £260 million. In February 1991 a Jewson-sponsored grant scheme was launched to help Football League clubs improve facilities. In the three years since its introduction 95 grants totalling £5.5 million have been awarded.

Despite the improvements with the help of grants, the fight against all-seater stadia has continued both inside and outside the game. In January 1992 an all-party parliamentary committee, headed by Tom Pendry MP, recommended that terracing be allowed to remain at clubs in the (then) Third and Fourth Divisions. Prior to the elections that year both Labour and Conservative parties said that they would review the all-seater requirement if they were voted to power. In the summer of 1992, David Mellor, at that time Secretary of State for National Heritage, announced that Third and Fourth Division grounds could retain terracing. Any club promoted to the top two divisions was to be given three years within which to comply with the all-seater requirement.

In 1993 the Football Trust received over £36 million, two-thirds from the reduction in the pools betting levy and the remainder as a donation from the pools companies from their Spot-The-Ball competitions. The Trust awards grants to help clubs with major works, such as seating, roofing and safety measures. These have ranged in size from £16,200 to help Hartlepool United install seats in their Rink Stand to £2 million for the redevelopment of the Leazes End at Newcastle United.

Unfortunately there have been cases of abuse. In November 1993 Bristol City were fined £40,000 and ordered to pay £8,000 in costs with respect to a claim made to the Football Trust. Leslie Kew, the club's former chairman and an FA councillor, was suspended from football activities for nine months and had to pay £2,000 costs. There are more recent threats to the Trust's income, however; namely the setting up of the national lottery and the increase in the number of people spending their money on fantasy leagues and play-by-mail competitions — none of which contribute to the Football Trust fund.

This book can only hope to present a snapshot picture of the changing face of Britain's football grounds. It is, however, one taken at the time of greatest change — a change, inspired by tragic events, which will have a profound effect on the future of the professional game itself.

Above: In the reduced capacity all-seater stadia of the 1990s, a season ticket is advisable for anyone wanting to watch the likes of Wolves' Kevin Keen.

Below: Standing room only at Leeds' Elland Road in 1967 – nowadays a thing of the past.

Daniel Ford & Michael Heatley
June 1994

Wembley Stadium

CAPACITY:

81,500

HIGHEST ATTENDANCE:

126,047 Bolton Wanderers v West Ham Utd, 28 April 1923, FA Cup Final

CAPACITY 1971:

100,000

There are larger stadiums in the world, most notably the Maracana Stadium in Brazil. There are more impressive structures in the world, most notably the Olympic Stadium in Munich. But there are few places that capture the atmosphere of football or have the same passion and excitement as Wembley when it is full.

Externally, Wembley looks much as it did when first opened in 1923. A sweep around the stadium will reveal a host of buildings and ramps that were not there 70 years or so ago, but the only visible sign that time moves on are plaques placed to commemorate the staging of the 1948 Olympics and 1966 World Cup. The only other modern intrusion is the presence of modern message boards which direct the visitor to the correct entrance.

From the air, Wembley has altered little since the roof was added to the entire stadium in 1963. Before then,

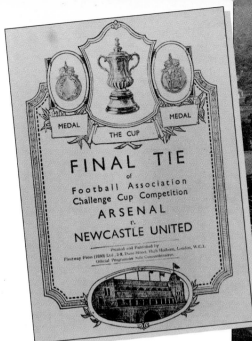

FINAL TIE

of

Football Association
Challenge Cup Competition

ARSENAL
v.
NEWCASTLE UNITED

only those sitting on either side were afforded any cover from the elements, and even those towards the front were guaranteed to get wet should the heavens decide to open during an event. The roof was built in 1963 at a cost of £500,000, using translucent fibreglass panels on the inner 36ft of roofing, giving Wembley a distinctive look and cover for all 100,000 patrons, of whom 44,000 were seated.

It is from the pitch, gazing around at the stadium, that changes becomes apparent. For a start, the stadium is now entirely seated, with coloured seats at each end depicting the Wembley/Tower logo. If we raise our eyes we will see the Olympic Gallery, a run of seating that appears at first glance to be dangled from the roof almost as an afterthought. In fact, the Olympic Gallery is Wembley's way of accepting that it would have to reduce its capacity once it became all-seater, but also utilising every available space to provide further accommodation. The Olympic Gallery runs around the entire stadium, broken only by a row of executive boxes on the Royal Box side and the television gantry and studio on the other. The view from the Olympic Gallery is certainly impressive, unless you are unfortunate enough to purchase a ticket immediately behind the huge scoreboards at either end. From these disadvantage points, the ball regularly

disappears from sight. The facilities in this little world within Wembley are also a great improvement on those which sufficed not ten years ago — fast food outlets have become the norm, but they do allow the maximum number of sales to be carried out expediently.

In recent years it is the seats that have provided Wembley with most of its criticism. Certainly, the view at pitch level is an awkward one, made all the more so by the presence of fencing which, if good behaviour became the norm rather than the exception, could be removed thereby eradicating one of

Opposite: Pre-match parachutists as Wembley stages the Coca Cola Cup Final.

Top: Seen under construction in 1922, Wembley immediately became the FA Cup Final venue.

Top left: The Cup Final programme from 1932, including an artist's impression.

Above: A dramatic view of Wembley's all-seater configuration in the 1990s.

FINAL TIE

OF THE
FOOTBALL
ASSOCIATION
CHALLENGE CUP
COMPETITION

AT THE

Empire Stadium
Wembley

SATURDAY, APRIL 25th, 1936

ARSENAL
v.
SHEFFIELD UNITED
Kick-off 3 p.m.

OFFICIAL PROGRAMME SIXPENCE

Wembley's main problems. It is also true to say that the seats at either end are far removed from the action, but this was the case when Wembley was built — short of getting FIFA to extend the length of a football pitch to 200yd there is little that Wembley or anyone else can do to change that!

It is under the seating that Wembley has undergone its greatest face-lift, one that has brought the stadium kicking and screaming into the 1990s. For many years Wembley was an embarrassment, both to its owners and its patrons, in the lack of facilities that were available in the ground. The toilets were little more than disgraceful,

the food facilities virtually non-existent unless you arrived when the doors opened, and the concourse, which runs around the entire stadium, was quickly transformed into a wet and rubbish-strewn disgrace. While the entire stadium is a long way from being ideal, the owners have spent considerable sums bringing the facilities and amenities up to date.

Wembley faces a great many challenges in the years to come, not least of which is familiarity breeding contempt. Up until 1951, Wembley might stage one or two major football matches a year — the FA Cup Final and one international. Since 1951,

Wembley has been home to England; since 1967, the League Cup Final; since 1974, the FA Charity Shield; since the early 1980s, the Autoglass Trophy; since the late 1980s, the Football League play-offs; since 1991, the FA Cup semi-finals; and since 1993, the Anglo-Italian Trophy. With each passing year a further competition seems to have Wembley host its final or semi-final, and in recent years supporters of some clubs have visited the stadium as many as six times in little more than a year. The by-product of this, in recent years, has been the almost unthinkable — tickets available on the day of a major match. Along

with the abundance of football there have been a host of other activities taking place at the stadium, including pop concerts on a regular basis during the summer months, a visit from the Pope and other successful commercial ventures. The funds generated by pop concerts and other activities ensured the football fan would not have to bear the full cost of renovation.

It has long been suggested that the FA should look at building its own stadium, for at present it is in the middle of a 21-year lease agreement with the owners of Wembley Stadium and looking to generate funds of its own. Such thoughts are not new; almost every decade seems to bring along fresh hope that a new national stadium, one more centrally placed, might one day be built, but none of the plans ever gets off the drawing board. Another alternative is to buy Wembley from its owners.

Regardless of Wembley's future there is one undeniable fact — the grand old stadium is still the venue players from all over the world look forward to playing in and which this country's supporters enjoy visiting. Built on the site of Watkin's Folly, it is now the Disneyland of world football!

Opposite: Wembley from the air in 1923, the year of its first FA Cup Final, where an over-capacity crowd got out of hand. The scenes at this legendary 'White Horse' Final were not repeated at subsequent events like the 1936 meeting of Arsenal and Sheffield United (Inset).

Top: Wembley in 1981, at the start of a decade that saw it used for American Football as well as soccer, rugby and pop concerts.

Left: Liverpool meet West Ham United in the League Cup Final of that same year.

Hampden Park

CAPACITY:

38,000 (due to rise to 60,000 by 1997)

HIGHEST ATTENDANCE:

149,547, Scotland v England, 17 April 1937 (record British attendance)

CAPACITY 1971:

134,000

After nearly two years out of action, Hampden Park — Scotland's national football stadium — reopened for the friendly international between Scotland and Holland on 23 March 1994. The giant sweeping bowl of terraces that once supported six-figure crowds has gone and Hampden is now a modern, if half-finished, 38,000 all-seater stadium. The capacity is planned to be 60,000 by the end of the century.

A government grant of £5 million was essential for the redevelopment programme, with £12 million spent on roofing and installing 22,400 seats on the two sides. The planned new 17,000-seater two-tier Main Stand will cost a further £12 million. Seating colours are mainly red and blue, although selected white seats pick out the word 'Hampden' on the side, while at the end blue and white seats are combined to display the Scottish flag.

Hampden Park was opened in 1903, its original title being the Third Hampden Park, as Queen's Park, the club side who own the ground, had used two grounds previously of the same name. The ground was officially opened on 31 October 1903 by Sir John Ure Primrose, the Lord Provost of Glasgow, before a Division One match in which Queen's Park beat Celtic 1-0. There were two separate South Stands, divided by a pavilion and three sides of open terracing, forming an oval-shaped ground.

The original pavilion was lost to fire two years after the opening, and this was replaced twice before the start of World War 1. Extra terracing for 25,000 was laid in 1927 and the North Stand built ten years later. The foresight paid dividends as Hampden

Park was to set a mind-boggling number of attendance records during the next few years.

The British record was established on 17 April 1937 when 149,547 paid to see the Scotland v England international, although it is estimated that as many as 160,000 actually saw the game. The Aberdeen v Celtic

Scottish Cup Final, just seven days later, attracted 146,433 — the highest for a match between two British club sides. The total of 143,570 for the Rangers v Hibernian Scottish Cup semi-final in 1948 remains the highest for a match other than a final.

Records are not confined to these shores. On 15 April 1970 some 136,505 watched Celtic v Leeds in a European Cup semi-final, to set a new European competition record. Even the record

Opposite: Hampden Park pictured just before its re-emergence as an international footballing venue in March 1994.

Left: The view from pitch level later that same year, showing some of the 38,000 seats. A further 22,000 are to be added later in the decade.

Below: Hampden Park in 1951 was neither all-seated nor covered to any great extent, but had a six-figure capacity.

attendance for a friendly in this country is held by Hampden Park. The official opening of the floodlights on 17 October 1960 attracted an amazing 104,494 to see Rangers take on Germany's Eintracht Frankfurt. Queen's Park's biggest attendance of 95,772 (v Rangers, 18 January 1930) is higher than any English club's record.

Hampden Park was the largest stadium in the world until 1950, when the Maracana was built in Rio de Janeiro, Brazil. The same year the South American stadium established the

highest ever attendance for a football match (199,589, Brazil v Uruguay).

In 1967 the West Terrace at Hampden Park was covered, but after more than 60 years as Scotland's showpiece ground it was in desperate need of refurbishment. Despite promises from all sides of the political spectrum for help during the 1970s it was not until over £2 million was raised from a public appeal, and a grant from the Football Trust secured, that finance was raised. In the early 1980s the North Stand was pulled down, part of the East Terrace removed and turnstiles installed, plus new toilets, safety barriers and food bars erected.

Hampden Park remains a sporting anomaly. A national stadium which has hosted World and European Cup internationals, top European Finals and set numerous attendance records for the nation remains home to an amateur club side playing in the lowest reaches of the domestic league. The stadium that seats thousands normally attracts crowds of just a few hundred to see the home games of Queen's Park. Despite their modern mediocrity, Scotland's oldest club and Scottish Cup winners on 10 occasions remains the guardian of Scotland's premier international venue.

Above: A full house for a New Year's Day fixture in 1978 contrasts with the rather smaller numbers arriving each weekend to see Queen's Park in the Scottish League.

Right: The West Terrace roof, source of the world-famous 'Hampden Roar', is clearly visible in this 1972 shot of the ground. Its addition five years earlier was one of the major alterations prior to the all-seater development of the 1990s.

Cardiff National Stadium

CAPACITY:

51,898

HIGHEST ATTENDANCE:

39,841 v Romania,
17 November 1993,
World Cup Qualifier

CAPACITY 1971:

100,000

Since the introduction of legislation designed to make football grounds a safer place to visit, the Welsh FA have been forced to turn their backs on the club grounds in the Principality and play their internationals at the National Stadium in Cardiff. If there are those who bemoan the move to what will always be regarded as the home of

Welsh rugby, then they would do well to remember that Wales played football internationals at the Arms Park, as it was known for many a year, between 1896 and 1910, when the stadium was perhaps, along with Wrexham, the only one large enough to accommodate the crowds wishing to see the matches against England and Scotland. Additionally, FIFA's decree on all-seater stadia being the only venues able to host World Cup and European Championship matches has meant that the National Stadium is the only stadium in Wales that meets this criterion; the National Stadium is therefore something of a must as far as football in Wales is concerned.

The stadium itself is one of the most impressive in the world, regardless of whether you are watching the oval code or the soccer variety. A cantilevered

roof provides perfect cover for spectators on three sides of the ground — the remaining end is left open deliberately to allow for natural ventilation of the pitch and because a roof at this end would reduce light to the adjacent buildings. It also helps the atmosphere to a vast extent; the passion for which rugby supporters are renowned has been recaptured on more than a few football occasions, with the sound whipping around the ground.

The most recent development at the ground has been the introduction of seating at the lower levels of the three sides covered by the roof. The open end remains unseated, which means for matches which fall under FIFA or UEFA jurisdiction this cannot be used, since neither body allows terracing. However, for rugby matches, be they World Cup or the Five Nations

The only other problem at the National Stadium is the pitch — and while the length and texture of the turf is not an important consideration in rugby, it is a vital one for football. The dilemma, therefore, is whether the National Stadium should make alterations purely for rugby, purely for football, or with an eye on both. That is a matter for the Welsh authorities to ponder.

Opposite left: Wales' premier sports venue as seen from the air in 1929.

Opposite right: Viewed nearly half a century later in 1977, much construction work is evident.

Above: By 1984, development was complete, one end having been left open for ventilation of the pitch.

Below: A fan's eye view of the National Stadium in 1993, the same year a fatal accident marred a World Cup qualifying tie.

Championship, the terracing can be used. This anomaly presents something of a problem. Recently, the change in fortunes in Welsh soccer on the pitch has meant that only the National Stadium has been large enough to accommodate those wishing to watch the games, but might the attendances have been even higher if all four ends had been available? There again, events at the end of the Romanian World Cup qualifier, when a rocket was fired across the stadium and killed one

spectator, have shown that even making everybody sit down at a soccer match is no guarantee that it will be trouble-free.

The National Stadium in Cardiff is certainly impressive but suffers from much the same logistical problems as any other major sporting venue. It might well be a peculiarly British problem, but there seems to be nowhere in the country that has yet eradicated the crush around the toilets immediately before, at half-time and immediately after the game.

Arsenal

CAPACITY:

38,500

HIGHEST ATTENDANCE:

**73,295 v Sunderland,
9 March 1935, Division One**

CAPACITY 1971:

63,000

Highbury's strangest ever supporters were those to be seen on the North Bank in 1992. The giant mural (35ft high and 140ft long), which was erected at a cost of £150,000 to hide unsightly building works during the redevelopment of the North Bank at Arsenal, was one of football's more curious sights. The mural showed an 8,000-strong 'crowd' and amplifiers were also used to generate mock cheering.

When it was initially erected it caused anger among supporters because the 'crowd' was made up entirely of white faces — a surprising oversight for a club with a strikingly multi-racial team.

This was quickly remedied with a few extra brush strokes and when the multi-racial supporters were finally removed the latest piece of the jigsaw in Highbury's £22 million redevelopment (partly funded by a controversial debenture scheme) was unveiled. The Group for the Alternative Arsenal Stand, formed by local residents, achieved some success in persuading the club to alter their original plan for the stand after getting an architect to

draw up an alternative design.

Seating was also installed at the Clock End during 1993. Yet the beginnings of this new future for Highbury had been unveiled there in the first stage of redevelopment in May 1989. Although despised by some on the terrace, the upgrade, which had started in the summer of 1988, included 48 money-spinning executive boxes, built in two layers and tucked under the newly erected roof. Also part of the complex was a new training hall, replacing the JVC-sponsored indoor training centre, plus offices, restaurant and conference facilities. The much bemoaned corporate supporter had staked a further claim to Highbury.

It was also at the end of the 1980s that Arsenal replaced and upgraded the seating throughout the ground, first experimented with a giant video screen and installed two electronic scoreboards.

Opposite: The famous North Bank mural obscured redevelopment during the 1992-93 season, but was criticised for its lack of racial multiplicity.

Above: A capacity crowd enjoys an FA Cup tie between Portsmouth and Aston Villa in March 1929. In recent years, Wembley has taken precedence as a semi-final venue.

Inset above: The Highbury of the 1990s includes a giant video screen.

The Clock End, like so much at Arsenal, owes its history to the club's renowned manager, Herbert Chapman. It was he who had a 45-minute clock erected on the North Stand in the early 1930s, but when that clock (since replaced by a traditional hour clock following objections from the FA) had to be moved because of building work in 1935 the timepiece gave its name to its new home at the south end of the ground.

Arsenal moved to Highbury in time for the 1913-14 season, leaving behind the Manor Ground at Plumstead, which had been their home for the previous 20 years.

Archibald Leitch, whose hand influenced so many of Britain's stadia, was brought in to design the new ground, which was situated on the playing fields belonging to St John's College of Divinity. The three open sides of terracing were dominated by the main stand, with each of its nine gables which faced the pitch spelling out a different letter of the club's name — 'ARSENAL FC'. (This was a forerunner of clubs spelling out their names by means of coloured seats. The East Stand at Arsenal now spells out 'The Gunners' in white on red.)

It was the inspiration of Herbert Chapman, who arrived in 1925 fresh from leading Huddersfield to two League Championships and an FA Cup Final, that really transformed Highbury. His on-field success followed him to Arsenal and coincided with a fast-developing ground; a ground that, until the 1989 changes, had stayed essentially intact.

Local residents were invited to dump their rubbish at the ground in 1931, to help increase the banking — but the

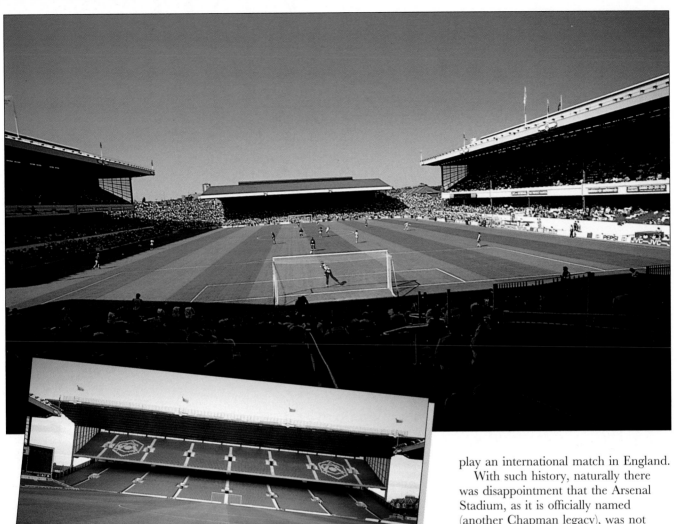

stadium that emerged was nothing like its unlikely base. A new West Stand erected at a cost of £45,000 was opened by HRH Prince Edward on 10 December 1932, four years and a day before his abdication as King.

Herbert Chapman died in 1934, but his legacy remained. Five League titles in that decade (in 1930-31 Arsenal became the first ever southern Champions), and three Wembley Cup Finals established Arsenal as England's leading club. A roof for the North Bank in 1935 and a new East Stand, similar to the stand it faced, a year later, gave Arsenal a ground to match their team.

World War 2 brought unlikely developments with a barrage balloon flown from the pitch, and the ground used as an air-raid centre and to house casualties. Arsenal were forced to move briefly to White Hart Lane when bombs fell on the North Bank (the roof was rebuilt in 1954) and the training pitch.

Highbury's proud international history was established long before the war began. It staged its first international, England v Wales, on 19 March 1920 and when Belgium visited the ground three years later they became the first foreign opposition to play an international match in England.

With such history, naturally there was disappointment that the Arsenal Stadium, as it is officially named (another Chapman legacy), was not chosen as a venue for the European Championships in 1996.

The changes in recent years have maintained Highbury as a leading ground in the UK, but with nearby Wembley a natural choice, the European Championship decision can be seen as a geographical one.

Opposite top: An interior view of Arsenal's North Bank Stand – somewhat more modern than the traditional marble halls.

Opposite: Highbury in 1949 showed a reduced capacity when compared with pre-war years. Note the North Bank, furthest from the camera, whose roof was only rebuilt in 1954.

Top: The view from the Clock End towards the North Bank in 1992 and (Above) the stand that replaced the latter's terracing.

Aston Villa

CAPACITY:

27,000

HIGHEST ATTENDANCE:

76,588 v Derby County,
2 March 1946, FA Cup 6th Round

CAPACITY 1971:

65,244

With a manager as ebullient as Ron Atkinson, it is perhaps fitting that Aston Villa grace a ground that was once the site of the Aston Lower Grounds amusement park. The club made its home there for the second and final time in 1897, after an absence of 17 years, at a cost of £250 rent a year, with the option to buy at five shillings a square yard within 21 years. All amusement facilities in time were removed or adapted, with the offices replacing the aquarium, skating rink and restaurant, the Witton Lane Stand covering the sub-tropical garden and a

lake being transformed into the pitch. The resulting Villa Park stadium remains today, albeit in substantially altered form.

The cycle track, which had been used for major events and to accommodate more spectators, was removed in the summer of 1914. The Witton Lane Stand was extended and banking at both ends increased.

The Trinity Road Stand, thought to have been originally designed by Archibald Leitch, arrived in 1922, with the next major development — the building up of the Holte End banking

Opposite: With a capacity of over 75,000, Villa Park was well placed to profit from the post World War 2 attendance boom. The Holte End, furthest from the camera, is particularly packed.

Below: Enlarging the Witton Lane Stand in the summer of 1914 to extend across the cycle track.

— finishing a few months after the declaration of World War 2. During the war years, the Trinity Road Stand was refitted as an air-raid shelter and a rifle company resided in the home team's dressing room.

Little changed in the immediate postwar period: the Holte End was covered in 1962, the better to funnel the home support's cheers on to the playing area, and two years later the Witton Lane roof was replaced by a plain sloping structure.

With the staging of World Cup games in 1966 came the conversion of the Witton Lane Stand to an all-seater, the extension of the pitch by three yards and the erection of 6,250 temporary seats on the uncovered Witton End banking. Villa spent a total of £99,000 on these redevelopments, but were granted £45,000 of this by the government.

In the late 1970s, the still-uncovered Witton End was replaced by a new North Stand which brought with it a police investigation when an independent report published in 1982 found Villa had paid 10% over the going rate and normal building procedures had not been followed.

After the stand was built, the pitch suffered from a lack of ventilation, forcing a new pitch to be laid. This, however, had its fair share of problems and a plastic cover, unfurled mechanically, was housed behind hoardings on the perimeter wall and used on the occasion of heavy rain.

Along with Hillsborough, Villa Park had long been a ground favoured for FA Cup semi-final fixtures, and the club moved quickly after the Taylor Report to maintain their position of pre-eminence. In the 1990s the New Witton Lane Stand, rebuilt as a two-tier stand at a cost of £5 million, was named after chairman H. D. 'Doug' Ellis.

At the end of the 1993-94 season the Holte End terrace — for so long the site of Villa's most vocal terrace fans — was demolished to make way for a two-tier stand to make Villa Park an all-seater stadium to comply with the Taylor Report. The loss of the Holte End standing reduced capacity from 45,016 to 27,000, though this was subsequently due to increase to 40,000 when work was completed. Despite Wembley muscling in on the semi-final scene, Villa Park remained an impressive if unamusing edifice.

Opposite top: The entrance to the Trinity Road Stand, built in 1922 and still going strong over half a century later.

Above: The new North Stand, pictured in 1983, replaced the uncovered Witton End.

Left: Villa entertain Fulham in 1967, the year after the ground was modified for use as a World Cup venue.

25

Birmingham City

CAPACITY:

25,500 (on completion of Tilton Road and Spion Kop redevelopment)

HIGHEST ATTENDANCE:

66,844 v Everton, 11 February 1939, FA Cup 5th Round

CAPACITY 1971:

52,500

The Taylor Report recommendations weighed most heavily on clubs like Birmingham City. A yo-yo existence between First and Second Division maintained interest and support, but did little for the long-term planning of St Andrews. In 1986, relegation from the top flight was not followed by a subsequent return and in 1989 the club dropped into the Third Division for the first time in its history. City, both team and ground, were firmly in the 'sleeping giant' category.

They had been left with the legacy of a large inner-city stadium with huge

tracts of sweeping terraces, yet a return to the First Division in 1992 put them back within the scope of Taylor's all-seater requirement. The fans' ambitions demanded that money be spent on a team capable of taking them back to the top; Taylor's Report demanded an all-seater stadium.

Birmingham were not obliged to go all-seater until August 1995, but new owner David Sullivan wanted to push ahead during the summer of 1994. Redevelopments include single-tier stands at the Tilton Road End (4,500 seats) and Spion Kop (9,500 seats plus

Opposite: St Andrews in 1978, looking down towards the Railway End.

Left: View from the terraces in 1947, shortly before the Main Stand was rebuilt.

Below left: The view from pitch level in 1979 showing the typical sweeping terraces of the pre-Taylor era. Note the central half-time scoreboard, now also a thing of the past.

24 executive boxes). Plans for the redevelopment of the Main Stand are dependent on the outcome of discussions on the long-term relocation of the club.

Birmingham moved to St Andrews, previously a piece of industrial wasteland, in 1906. A record 66,844 crammed into the ground for an FA Cup 5th Round tie with Everton just months before the start of World War 2 — and, later, the Blitz.

German bombers devastated St Andrews by hitting it 20 times; then the Main Stand was destroyed in 1942 by a freak fire, forcing Birmingham to move in briefly with their neighbours at Villa Park.

The Main Stand was rebuilt in the 1950s; terracing to the south and west were covered on the back of continuous Inter City Fairs Cup (forerunner of the UEFA Cup) involvement from 1955-61 (runners-up twice), and the City Stand (north) was erected a decade later.

In recent years St Andrews will be remembered for the riots on 11 May 1985. On that day a 12ft-high boundary wall collapsed, following rioting from Leeds fans, killing a 15-year-old supporter who had been attending his first professional game and injuring 96 police officers. Coming the same day as the tragic fire at Valley Parade, the combination of events prompted the Popplewell Report.

Blackburn Rovers

CAPACITY:

31,000

HIGHEST ATTENDANCE:

61,783 v Bolton Wanderers,
2 March 1929,
FA Cup 6th Round

CAPACITY 1971:

52,000

Just as the millions of benefactor Jack Walker enabled manager Kenny Dalglish to transform Blackburn into 1990s title contenders, so Ewood Park was renewed — though success dictated that this was done in sections to ensure the least possible loss of seating.

Success had also preceded Rovers' adoption of the ground in 1890 when, following their fourth FA Cup win, they spent £1,000 on reconstruction of Ewood Park before their first game against Accrington in September. That Christmas, they had their first taste of crowd trouble when Darwen fans tore up goalposts and smashed dressing room windows after Rovers fielded a depleted first team. Further trouble occurred six years later when part of a stand holding a 20,000 crowd collapsed: fortunately, there were no fatalities and only five people were injured.

The early part of the century saw many improvements: designed by Archibald Leitch, the Nuttall Street Stand was built for £24,000, while the Riverside Stand, erected between their two Championship wins of 1912 and

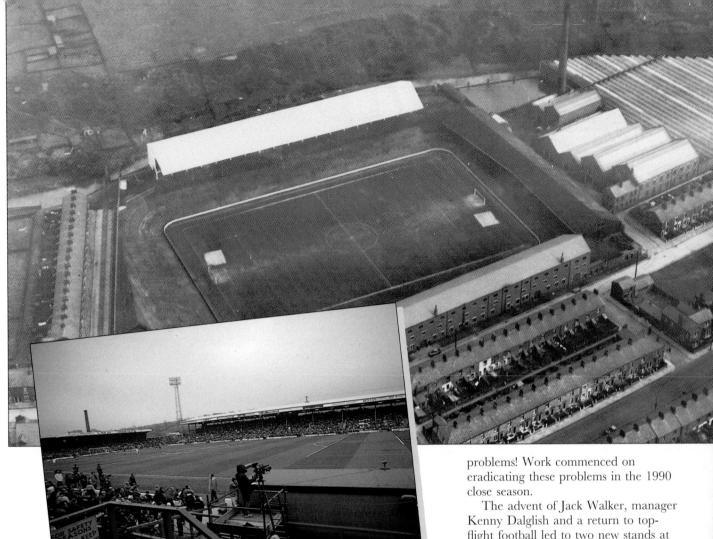

1914, brought Ewood Park's capacity to 70,866, including 7,000 seats. 1928 saw the wooden perimeter railing replaced by a concrete wall, the Riverside Stand re-roofed and the Blackburn End terraced.

Funds raised on the way to a Wembley FA Cup appearance in 1960 enabled the construction of a concrete cantilever roof on the Blackburn End terrace, thus ensuring all four sides of the ground were covered.

Fire broke out in the Nuttall Street Stand in July 1984 and it is likely that the damage would have been more extensive had improvements not been carried out following the 1975 Safety of Sports Grounds Act. As it was, Rovers rebuilt the stand incorporating a new block of executive boxes and a glass-fronted lounge. Named the John Lewis Complex after the club's founder, this development was completed at a cost of £250,000.

In the aftermath of the Bradford fire, structural problems were revealed during safety checks of the Riverside Stand and it was demolished in 1987 and replaced by a 700-seat structure incorporating a special section for disabled fans.

Next in line for redevelopment was the playing surface: in 1989 the pitch was dug up and a revolutionary 'Techturf' pitch laid. Based on natural grass growing through Netlon meshing, this was said to have many of the benefits of artificial pitches — but on 7 October 1989 Rovers were the only team in the League to have a waterlogged pitch following drainage problems! Work commenced on eradicating these problems in the 1990 close season.

The advent of Jack Walker, manager Kenny Dalglish and a return to top-flight football led to two new stands at the Blackburn and Darwen Ends, each of 8,000 capacity: erection began in early 1993. This extensive building work restricted capacity to 21,273, but when finished would allow approximately 31,000 to watch Rovers in all-seater comfort.

Opposite top: A 1971 view towards the corner of the ground where the Blackburn End and Riverside Stand meet.

Opposite: 1993 saw the building of a new Darwen End stand, pictured here during construction.

Top: An aerial view of Ewood Park in 1928. The Blackburn End (left of the picture) was the last side of the ground to be covered and did not receive a roof until the 1960s.

Above left: The new Riverside Stand (opposite) replaced its predecessor after structural problems were found during a post-Bradford fire survey.

Blackpool

CAPACITY:

10,337

HIGHEST ATTENDANCE:

39,118 v Manchester Utd,
19 April 1952,
Division One

CAPACITY 1971:

38,000

While there are numerous clubs whose fortunes have dipped considerably since the 1960s, few have fallen as far from grace as Blackpool. And fortunes on the field are reflected by a ground sadly in decline, though millionaire chairman Owen Oyston announced plans to groundshare in the 1994-95 season as a purpose-built, multi-function home for the club took shape.

Bloomfield Road was first developed in 1899, with the current West Stand surviving from that time. Aside from necessary safety and structural repairs, this stand appears today almost as it did then. The South Stand is slightly younger, having been constructed in 1925 and housing offices and player facilities. The final side, the east, dates from the late 1930s when a roof was raised over the current East Paddock.

Saddest of all at Blackpool is the loss of the Kop at the north end of the ground. This once-proud structure was home to Blackpool's own supporters; now barely half of it is open and it accommodates the visitors with no cover, and the barest of facilities. Displaced Kop punters have been accommodated by removal of the seats in the Paddock.

Bloomfield Road's future has long been in doubt, previous attempts by the club to rebuild the West Stand having constantly fallen at the planning stage. Until 1994, a move to a new stadium seemed the only viable alternative.

Top: In 1951, Bloomfield Road accommodated Blackpool's most vocal supporters in the uncovered Spion Kop.

Above: A 1971 view across the pitch to the East Paddock during a game against Hull.

Left: Blackpool's most famous attraction towers over the West Stand.

BLOOMFIELD ROAD

Bolton Wanderers

CAPACITY:

20,500

HIGHEST ATTENDANCE:

69,912 v Manchester City,
18 February 1933,
FA Cup 5th Round

CAPACITY 1971:

60,136

Bolton's discussions on a move to a new ground in the 1990s could put Burnden Park out of sporting service after nearly a century of use. Wanderers moved to the site in 1895, 21 years after their formation, and in 1901 hosted the FA Cup Final replay between Tottenham and Sheffield United.

Soon afterwards work was started on the Main Stand. This was extended during World War 1, and at the same time the Great Lever Stand was covered. The Burnden Stand replaced the Darcy Lever Stand at the end of the 1920s and this was used for storing food during World War 2. It was still in service for the Ministry of Supply when, while playing Stoke on 9 March 1946, 33 people were killed in a crush after thousands of supporters poured through turnstiles and over gates at the

Embankment. One of the major sporting tragedies in this country, it prompted a major safety rethink and a voluntary licensing system was set up for larger grounds.

Bolton carried out a series of safety improvements, but major ground changes did not come until 1979 when seats were installed in the Great Lever

Stand. In 1986 part of the famous open terracing at the Railway Embankment was demolished to make way for a supermarket, giving the north corner of the ground a plain brick façade. The Great Lever Stand was re-roofed during the 1993-94 season but further redevelopment hinges on the outcome of discussions for the club's long-term relocation.

Above: The Burnden Stand, pictured in 1991, was built at the end of the 1920s.

Left: Seen in 1974, the Great Lever Stand (right) was seated in 1979 and re-roofed during the 1993-94 season.

Bradford City

CAPACITY:

14,387

HIGHEST ATTENDANCE:

**39,146 v Burnley,
11 March 1911,
FA Cup 4th Round**

CAPACITY 1971:

24,000

Prior to May 1985, Valley Parade Bradford had little to distinguish it from a score or more of provincial football grounds. The home of Bradford City since 1903, it was situated close to trams and trains and boasted an Archibald Leitch-designed Main Stand (seating 5,300) and a Midland Road standing terrace for 8,000 with a clock on its centre gable. The total capacity of 30,000 was admirable for a pre-World War 1 football club and Cup winners but, by the 1980s Valley Parade was showing its age, like so many grounds of its era.

The Midland Road Stand had been sold to Berwick Rangers in 1952 and a smaller stand erected in its place, but this too was rebuilt in 1960. The Main or South Parade Stand had endured since the ground was first used in the late 19th century as a rugby venue.

Finances were tight, and the club's continuing absence from the top flight ensured that money remained in short supply: groundstaff were employed to cover the Midland Road standing area in late 1969, while the ground spent most of the 1970s in the ownership of Bradford Corporation to whom it was

Opposite: View from the Main Stand looking towards the Midland Road Stand. Compare the changing skyline (Left), taken just a few years earlier in 1978.

Below: Valley Parade in 1966; the Bradford End is covered but occupants of the Spion Kop still had to brave the elements.

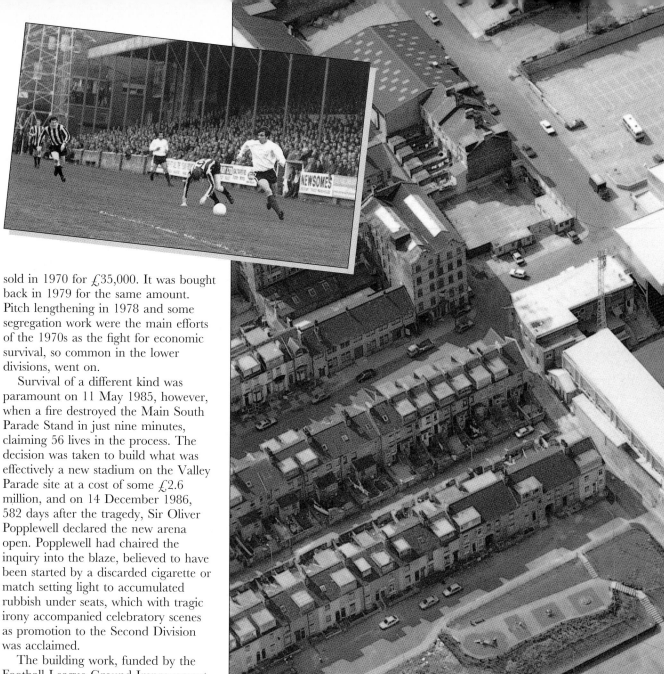

sold in 1970 for £35,000. It was bought back in 1979 for the same amount. Pitch lengthening in 1978 and some segregation work were the main efforts of the 1970s as the fight for economic survival, so common in the lower divisions, went on.

Survival of a different kind was paramount on 11 May 1985, however, when a fire destroyed the Main South Parade Stand in just nine minutes, claiming 56 lives in the process. The decision was taken to build what was effectively a new stadium on the Valley Parade site at a cost of some £2.6 million, and on 14 December 1986, 582 days after the tragedy, Sir Oliver Popplewell declared the new arena open. Popplewell had chaired the inquiry into the blaze, believed to have been started by a discarded cigarette or match setting light to accumulated rubbish under seats, which with tragic irony accompanied celebratory scenes as promotion to the Second Division was acclaimed.

The building work, funded by the Football League Ground Improvement Trust, insurance money and the club's own resources, was completed as the team played in temporary exile at the Odsal Rugby League Stadium. It resulted in a magnificent new Main Stand, with 5,000 seats considerably larger than its ill-fated predecessor and with a framework of prefabricated steel trusses and concrete roof members. Elsewhere, the reconcreted, covered Kop held 7,000 while closed-circuit television and electronically controlled turnstiles responding to crowd size and strength were among the state-of-the-art improvements.

Exit gates in the perimeter fences were also built in, though the fences were soon to be lowered nationwide in the aftermath of another disaster at Hillsborough. A memorial to those who lost their lives in the 1985 fire was erected on the outer wall of the new Main Stand, at the spot where a floral shrine had previously lain.

Though it would never again approach its record attendance established shortly before World War 1, the new Valley Parade's total capacity of 14,387 (some 6,500 of which were seated) enabled the followers of the Second Division outfit to watch their team in relative comfort and, most importantly, safety.

Opposite: The Main South Parade Stand pictured in 1971, and (Left) in 1978, was destroyed in just nine minutes in the 1985 fire which claimed 56 lives.

Above: Bradford City's Valley Parade ground in the 1990s, with covered Spion Kop (left) and new Main Stand.

Brentford

CAPACITY:

13,870

HIGHEST ATTENDANCE:

**39,626 v Preston North End,
5 March 1938,
FA Cup 6th Round**

CAPACITY 1971:

38,000

Above: Griffin Park at pitch level in the late 1980s, looking across to the Brook Road End with the new Main Stand on the left and New Road terracing to the right.

Above right: Griffin Park in 1957, seen from a similar angle but a rather greater altitude.

In 1994 Griffin Park had the honour of hosting the first England match under new coach Terry Venables, an Under-21 international against Denmark. A crowd of 11,553 (a record for an Under-21 friendly) turned up to see Trevor Sinclair's goal get Venables off to a winning start a day before the seniors beat their Danish counterparts at Wembley.

Brentford moved to Griffin Park in 1904, their sixth ground since their formation 15 years earlier. During the interwar years the Main Stand was built and extended, and covers erected on the terraces on New Road and Brook Road.

In February 1983 a fire destroyed the Main Stand but its replacement was not opened until the start of the 1984-85 season. The small two-tiered Brook Road Stand was opened at the end of 1986, white seats spelling out the club's name in rows of red seats. In 1993 the East Terrace was redeveloped at a cost of £250,000 in preparation for seating that part of the ground.

Brighton & Hove Albion

CAPACITY:

17,607

HIGHEST ATTENDANCE:

36,747 v Fulham,
27 December 1958,
Division Two

CAPACITY 1971:

38,000

Running three-quarters of the length of the pitch, the Goldstone Ground's West Stand remains something of an enigma. Indeed, the entire west side was very much a riddle during Brighton's brief sojourn in the then First Division in the late 1970s and early 1980s. A temporary stand was built alongside the permanent West Stand, seating an extra 974 and having the look and feel of being constructed out of left-over building materials; indeed, it was known unofficially as the Lego Stand during its brief life.

Opposite the West Stand is the East Side terracing, one corner of which accommodates the visiting supporters. The view from this corner is among the worst in the Football League, for the banking is not quite deep enough to enable an unhindered view of the proceedings on the pitch.

Brighton's own vociferous followers are to be found in the North Stand which received a new roof in the mid-1980s that provides more than adequate cover for its patrons. At the opposite end of the ground, a lower roof covers the South Stand, which is all-seater.

Above right: The cramped confines of the Goldstone Ground in 1993 with a car park and Portakabins where a second, temporary West Stand used to be.

Right: The view at pitch level in 1975, looking across to the East Terrace.

As with many clubs, Brighton & Hove Albion would like to move to a brand new purpose-built stadium but lack the finances to do so. There is an additional drawback to the Goldstone Ground in that the lease, held by the local council, stipulates that no structure can be built on the site higher than 50ft above pitch level in order not to reduce the view of the houses alongside the ground. Since this has remained the case since 1926, the locals have had a completely uninterrupted view of the Goldstone Ground for near on 70 years!

37

Bristol City

Ashton Gate looked likely to become home to both Bristol clubs when Rovers were forced to leave Eastville in 1986. A dispute over rent ended that scenario, and while Rovers still search for a new ground from their temporary home at Bath their city rivals continue their upgrade of facilities to meet the demands of the Taylor Report.

The new all-seater stand at the north of the ground, with work taking place in the summer of 1994, replaces the last remaining open terracing at Ashton Gate. Three years previously, new seats and a roof were added to the Main Stand, 2,911 seats were put into the enclosure and 6,005 seats were installed in the Covered End (south end).

Ashton Gate has been home to City since 1904. The covered terrace went up in the 1920s and the Main Stand was completed in the 1950s, partly funded by compensation from the War Damages Commission after a bomb damaged a stand in 1941. The Dolman Stand opposite was opened in 1970, but spiralling costs left the club with a heavy debt which, exacerbated by a drop from First to Fourth Division in consecutive seasons, left the club on the brink of extinction in 1982.

A deal for a groundshare with Rovers was struck (the two clubs had shared briefly in 1980 after a fire at Eastville), but rental terms could not be agreed and Ashton Gate remained the sole preserve of City.

CAPACITY:

20,000

HIGHEST ATTENDANCE:

43,335 v Preston North End, 16 February 1935, FA Cup 5th Round

CAPACITY 1971:

40,000

Top: By 1993, only the Ashton Road End remained uncovered, the Dolman Stand (right) being opened in 1970.

Above left: Ashton Gate in 1933; the most conspicuous feature being the covered Winterstoke Road End, built in the late 1920s and funded by the sale of two players.

Left: The Main Stand, completed in the 1950s, was partly funded by the supporters' club.

Bristol Rovers

CAPACITY:

8,800

HIGHEST ATTENDANCE:

38,472 v Preston North End,
30 January 1960,
FA Cup 4th Round (Eastville),
9,646 v Liverpool,
8 February 1992,
FA Cup 4th Round (Twerton Park)

CAPACITY 1971:

39,333 (Eastville)

Bristol Rovers' future remained as uncertain in 1994 as when they left Eastville eight years earlier. Nobody believed the deal to share Twerton Park with non-League Bath City was a long-term solution. However, fans were able to accept it as a necessary temporary measure when, in 1990, the club seemed to have struck a deal with the city council to relocate them at a new ground at a 150-acre site at Severnside to the west of the city. One hundred acres were planned to be used for a sports complex to help finance the neighbouring multi-purpose stadium. The relationship turned sour in July 1993 when the council decided against progressing with the scheme. Fans pointed out that the site had become valuable after the announcement that a new motorway (M49) would run alongside it.

Since Rovers' arrival in 1986, Twerton Park has undergone a number

of improvements including a new 236-seat family stand, new toilet block, new turnstiles, an electronic crowd monitor, a police control post, new crush barriers and the construction of a family enclosure.

Rovers spent 99 uncertain years at Eastville, the final game coming on 26 April 1986. In the end it was simply costing the club too much and the stadium owners cared little as Rovers' rent was only a fraction of what they earned through other activities, mainly greyhound racing.

Top left: Eastville, Bristol Rovers' home for nearly a century, pictured in 1978, with dog track clearly visible in the foreground.

Above: With its sub-10,000 capacity, Bath City's Twerton Park ground offered a temporary refuge down the motorway in 1986 but had become a more permanent home by the time this photo was taken in 1993.

Burnley

CAPACITY:

21,565

HIGHEST ATTENDANCE:

54,775 v Huddersfield,
23 February 1924,
FA Cup 3rd Round

CAPACITY 1971:

39,000 (temporary during alterations)

The mere idea of non-League football at Turf Moor, home of Burnley, original members of the Football League, seems absurd. Yet, in 1987, the unthinkable almost became a reality. On 9 May, in what became known as 'The Orient Game', Burnley had to beat the Londoners to avoid relegation from the Football League. Even victory on that day may not have been enough; other results had to go in their favour. A gate of 17,600 (the average for the season was 3,360) crammed into Turf Moor to see football's God smile down on East Lancashire. Burnley won 2-1 while Lincoln City went down to Swansea and non-League football.

Burnley survived, but their plans for the ambitious redevelopment of Turf Moor now hinge on the club's ability to raise the necessary finance.

The scheme comprises plans to demolish the two terraced sections (Bee Hole and Longside) of the ground to make way for new two-tiered stands with associated restaurant and conference facilities and private boxes. Worked out with the Lobb Partnership of London, the plans would convert Turf Moor into a 20,000 all-seater stadium with an option of a further extension to 25,000. The extra seats would come from the expensive replacement of the Bob Lord Stand and Cricket Field Stand to mirror the new developments, or further seated rows could be added to the new stands.

Top: Serried ranks of terraced houses abut Turf Moor, pictured in 1929.

Above: The Cricket Field stand, visible to the left of this 1970 action, was completed the previous year.

Opposite top: This 1993 view reveals two terraced sides (one uncovered), but this is set to change.

Opposite: The scene in 1978 from the open, Bee Hole Lane End showing the Bob Lord (left) and Cricket Field Stands.

Burnley came to Turf Moor in 1883 (only Stoke City and Preston have been at their current grounds longer) and within three years were dubbed the Royalites when Prince Albert visited Turf Moor to see the match against Bolton.

During the next two decades two stands and terracing had emerged. In 1927 England and Wales battled out the only international match to be played at Turf Moor, with England selecting Burnley favourites Jack Hill and Louis Page to boost local support.

Prime Minister Edward Heath officially opened the Cricket Field Stand at Turf Moor on 23 November 1973, although it had been finished since 1969; and he was called upon again at the start of the next season to open the Bob Lord Stand (named after the chairman), a replacement for the Main Stand.

Cardiff City

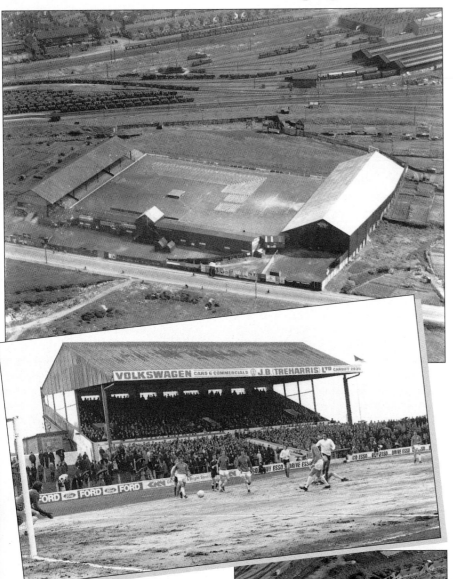

Having doubled since 1910 as the Welsh national team's home venue (a match against England in 1961 attracting the record ground attendance of 61,566), Ninian Park has recently proved too roomy for the lower division crowds Cardiff themselves attract.

Built on a former rubbish tip, with a £90 annual rent, Ninian Park was originally going to be called Sloper Park until Lord Ninian Crichton Stuart stepped in to guarantee finance. The ground opened with a friendly against Aston Villa in September 1910 and Scotland were the visitors for the first international a year later.

In 1920, the Canton Stand was built (a covered bank with bench seats) and the Bob Bank was covered, while eight years later a larger roof was built over the Grangetown End.

Two years before the outbreak of World War 2, the wooden Main Stand was burned down, apparently by thieves trying to blast open the club's safe, and was replaced by a superior brick and steel construction.

In 1958, the Bob Bank was extended, with a new roof built over the back section. Despite the Main Stand being extended to run the complete length of the pitch in 1973, Cardiff were severely hit by the findings of safety inspectors in 1977. The Grangetown End roof was demolished and banking cut back, reducing the capacity to just 10,000.

By the 1990s, the 3,500-capacity Main Stand was supplemented by the half-seated Popular Bank housing 5,300, with a total seating of 12,000 — more than sufficient for even the traditionally hard-fought derbies with local rivals Swansea City.

Top: Ninian Park in 1935, when both ends were covered.

Above left: The Main Stand in 1972, the year before it was extended to run the length of the pitch.

Left: By 1993, the Grangetown End had been uncovered for over a decade.

CAPACITY:

20,340

HIGHEST ATTENDANCE:

57,893 v Arsenal,
22 April 1953,
Division One

CAPACITY 1971:

58,000

Charlton Athletic

CAPACITY:

15,000

HIGHEST ATTENDANCE:

75,031 v Aston Villa,
12 February 1938,
FA Cup 5th Round

CAPACITY 1971:

66,000 (at the time the largest in
the Football League)

The saga of Charlton Athletic's return to the Valley will act as a constant reminder as to the strength of feelings that exist within the ranks of supporters. On 21 September 1985, a tearful and angry crowd of 8,858 thought they were witnessing the last game at the Valley. Demonstrations held the game up, while afterwards supporters cut turfs from the pitch for souvenirs.

Earlier that year the Greater London Council, following the Bradford fire and riot at Birmingham, had ordered the massive East Terrace to be closed for safety reasons. The catalyst for the move, however, was a two-acre site behind the West Stand which was used as a car park, toilets and main access to the ground.

Sunley Construction, Charlton's owners could do little when Adelong Ltd, owned by Michael Gliksten, the man from whom they had bought the club, decided to fence off this area of land. Gliksten had retained ownership of the ground when he sold the club and the site had not formed part of the negotiated lease.

Without the use of this crucial two-acre site Charlton's hand was forced and they eventually struck a groundsharing deal with Crystal Palace. The fans were dismayed. While they played their home games at Selhurst Park, some seven miles away, the Valley sat unused.

On the field, promotion to the First Division was gained in the very season the Valley had been left behind. (Ironically, Charlton's landlords Crystal Palace were in the Second Division at

Left: The Valley, pictured in 1961, nearly a quarter of a century before Charlton Athletic left Woolwich for a nomadic existence as lodgers of Crystal Palace and West Ham. The extensive South Bank terracing is the most clearly visible feature.

the time.) Four seasons later they were back down, but the campaign for the move back to the Valley remained all-consuming.

During the next seven years (Charlton shared with both Palace and West Ham) fans constantly and vociferously demanded a return to what they called the club's home.

Hopes of a return followed the purchase of Adelong Ltd by two of the club's directors, Roger Alwen and Michael Norris, in March 1988, but fans were forced to endure a series of false promises. Greenwich Council planners turned down plans for a super stadium and, in frustration, the fans united under the banner of the Valley Party. In the local elections in May 1990 the party gained almost 15,000 votes and succeeded in ousting the chair of planning on the council. A year later planners gave their approval to a revised scheme for the ground but it was not until supporters raised £1 million that the move could proceed.

Finally, after seven years (2,627 days to be exact) Charlton triumphantly returned 'home' when they played Portsmouth at the Valley on 5 December 1992. The East Terrace remained empty for the return; only three sides were open (including a temporary stand) and the capacity was a mere 8,000, but it mattered not as the fans saw their side mark the occasion with a victory. At the end of 1993 the club finally said goodbye to the giant East Terrace that had plagued them in recent years. The new East Stand, built with the help of a £1.4 million grant from the Football Trust and boasting 6,000 seats, was opened on 2 April 1994 for the Easter Saturday fixture against Southend.

Charlton first moved to the Valley, an unused chalk pit, in 1919, while they were still amateurs. Within two years the club had turned professional and been elected into the Third Division (South). The early League games would have been strange affairs because the Main Stand, terracing and other fittings associated with a football ground were not complete until 1922.

The return to the Valley in 1992 is certainly the most well documented — but it was not the first time that the club had 'come home'. In 1923 Charlton left the Valley to seek their fortune at Catford FC, near Millwall. They returned within a few months, after disastrous attendances, but it gave Valiants fans a taste of what was to come.

Opposite: The East Terrace was replaced in early 1994 by a magnificent new stand seating 6,000 and boosting the redeveloped ground's capacity to 15,000.

Opposite below: Charlton entertain South London neighbours Fulham in 1976, the multi-span roof of the West Stand (completed in 1922 at a cost of almost £20,000) clearly visible.

Below: The East Stand takes shape in 1993 as play goes on.

Bottom: The visit of Portsmouth on 5 December 1992 was Charlton's first 'home' game since 1985.

Chelsea

CAPACITY:
28,500

HIGHEST ATTENDANCE:
**82,905 v Arsenal,
12 October 1935,
Division One**

CAPACITY 1971:
60,000

Despite having staged sporting events since 1877, the future of Stamford Bridge hung in the balance when the club's lease terminated in 1989 and chairman Ken Bates rejected an option to buy the ground for £40 million.

It was a gamble that paid off, for property values declined and Chelsea were left *in situ*, being granted planning permission to erect three stands (seating 24,000) to accompany the existing East Stand. This also included provision for a 160-bedroom hotel and 264 flats, while refurbishment of the East Stand itself (never properly finished in the 1970s due to the club's poor financial situation) commenced in May 1991, resulting in a magnificent three-tier structure.

Archibald Leitch was the man commissioned in February 1905 to design Stamford Bridge's original East Stand, while material for terracing the other three sides of the ground came from the excavation of the Piccadilly Underground line and the Kingsway tramway tunnel.

The ground staged four England matches, the first in 1913 and the last in 1946, and was the venue for three FA Cup Finals between 1920 and 1922 as well as accommodating other sports such as athletics, rugby, baseball, midget car racing, rifle shooting, cricket and greyhound racing.

Stamford Bridge remained largely unchanged (the building of a North Stand had begun in the summer of 1939, but was never finished due to

World War 2) until 1965, when work on a stand on the west side commenced. This drastically reduced the capacity, with the 6,300 seats replacing 20,000 standing places.

Impressive plans to take the Bridge into the 21st century were unveiled in 1970, including a new British Rail station 100yd away, but these did not reach fruition. Leitch's East Stand was replaced, but with gates dwindling the cost proved prohibitive: the ground and club were separated, the former being run by SB Property. When this was taken over by Marler Estates in the early 1980s and property values rose,

eviction and groundsharing with Fulham or QPR seemed a real possibility until Ken Bates' dramatic intervention (he became chairman in 1982) restored hope to the West London club.

In 1994 work began on a two-tier, all-seater stand on the North Terrace (completion expected in November), while the new South and North Stands, both all-seater, were expected to be finished by the 1996-97 season. The Taylor Report had meant bidding goodbye to the Shed, haunt of the most vocal of Chelsea's terrace supporters, at the South End, but this was perhaps an acceptable price to pay for Stamford Bridge's continued existence.

Opposite top: Stamford Bridge at pitch level in 1967, with the massed ranks of standing fans familiar in the pre-Taylor era.

Opposite: The view from the air in 1935, with the dog track clearly apparent.

Top: Chelsea's East Stand, completed in 1991 after almost two decades of expensive development.

Above left: The Shed, seen here at top left in this 1958 picture, entertained its last standing fans in May 1994 (Above).

Chester City

CAPACITY:

6,000

HIGHEST ATTENDANCE:

20,500 v Chelsea,
16 January 1952, FA Cup
3rd Round replay (Sealand Road)

CAPACITY 1971:

18,300 (Sealand Road)

After two years groundsharing with non-League Macclesfield Town, Chester City moved into their new home, the Deva Stadium, at the end of 1992. The Stadium was the sixth ground Chester have used since they were formed in 1884, although most of their history is tied up with Sealand Road.

After Morrison Developments of Manchester purchased the Sealand Road site to develop it as a retail park in 1990, Chester moved into the Moss Rose Ground with their Conference neighbours while they waited for the new ground to be built.

On 5 September 1992, 4,981 people watched the home side beat Burnley 3-0 in the first game at the new stadium. Built on a greenfield site a mile and a half to the south-west of the city centre, the Deva Stadium is neat and uniform, with plenty of space for on-site car parking.

The North and South (away end) Stands behind the goals both provide terracing for 1,296 spectators. The East Stand (home) seats 2,134 with 40 disabled places, and the West Stand has seating for 1,274, including 32 disabled places. The club offices are located behind the East Stand.

When Chester moved to Sealand Road in 1906 it was, like their current home, surrounded only by fields, but gradually light industry was built up around it. The small wooden Main Stand remained in use until a decade before the retail developers moved in, when it was replaced by a new £500,000 stand. The covered terracing at the Sealand Road End for home supporters remained in use from the club's early days in the Football League (Chester replaced Nelson in 1931). The floodlights were erected in 1960 and first used for a League Cup tie with

Orient that same year. The Popular Stand, which stood opposite the Main Stand, was covered in 1968.

Chester's record attendance came in 1952 when 20,500 spectators crammed into Sealand Road for an FA Cup 3rd Round replay with Chelsea, but by the time the club left the ground almost 40 years later, safety measures had forced the capacity down to less than half of that figure.

Opposite: Skies are, appropriately, blue over Chester's Deva Stadium, the compact new home to which they moved in 1992.

Top: Sealand Road seen in the 1970s and (Above) 1980s. Neither decade saw success on the pitch, and it was the ground's potential for retail development that funded the club's move after two seasons lodging at Macclesfield.

Coventry City

CAPACITY:

22,500

HIGHEST ATTENDANCE:

51,455 v Wolves,
29 April 1967,
Division Two

CAPACITY 1971:

51,200

Coventry's modern Highfield Road stadium entered English football history in 1981 as its first all-seater stadium, pre-dating the Taylor Report by a number of years.

The club's association with Highfield Road began in 1899, when a 12-row stand was built on the King Richard Street site of a six and a half acre plot purchased from the Craven cricket club. The *Coventry Observer* described the stand as 'an ornament of which the committee might well be proud,' and it was joined after the successful 1910 season by a stand on the north side. A third, terrace stand was bought from Twickenham in 1927, and nine years later the original, now rotting, Main Stand of 1899 was replaced at a cost of £14,000 as the club purchased the Highfield Road freehold.

The north side stand was replaced in 1964 by the Sky Blue Stand, a double-decker West Stand joining it in 1967 as

the club won promotion to the top flight. The destruction of the Main Stand by fire was made good in the 1968 close season at the cost of only two home games postponed, but it was the 1981 decision to go all-seater that caused most controversy.

Some 8,000 extra seats were installed, reducing capacity from 36,500 to 20,600. Limited standing was reintroduced two years later. In the wake of Taylor, the decision was reached to return to all-seater, build a new stand at the Kop and and extend its roof to the Sky Blue Stand, the result being a 22,500-capacity stadium with cover for 95% of the crowd. The estimated cost of £6 million was partly defrayed by a £2 million grant from the Football Trust.

The Sky Blue Stand was duly covered in the summer of 1993, while the following year saw the construction of the East Stand with a capacity of nearly 5,000.

Opposite: Highfield Road viewed from the air in 1939 and (Above Left) in 1993.

Top: A packed house for an early-1980s visit of Manchester United.

Above: Looking out on the pitch in 1961, with the Main Stand visible to the right. Two decades later, Highfield Road would take English football into the all-seater age.

Crystal Palace

CAPACITY:

17,619

HIGHEST ATTENDANCE:

51,482 v Burnley,
11 May 1979,
Division Two

CAPACITY 1971:

51,000

When Crystal Palace and Charlton struck a deal to share Selhurst Park in September 1985 — the first ever groundsharing arrangement between League clubs — supporters nationwide could have been forgiven for thinking big changes were on the way.

Pundits had been saying for years that many football clubs could survive only if they pooled their resources; all it needed was someone to take that first step. But if the first domino had indeed fallen, it did not fall hard enough. Apart from a few notable exceptions most clubs, and supporters, refuse to accept a practice widely used elsewhere in the world. Clearly an English club's ground remains its castle.

Despite football's general scepticism, Crystal Palace remain forerunners in the groundsharing ideal, having accepted Wimbledon in 1991 as their second tenants. Ironically, at times, both Charlton and Wimbledon have brought a higher grade of football to Selhurst Park than Palace themselves.

The system, although still opposed by a small group of fans, has worked well for Palace. The deal with Charlton meant that they received 10% of their tenants' gate receipts, plus half the running costs. The deal with Wimbledon is worth £40,000 in rent plus some savings from staff sharing.

The ground itself clearly benefited from the extra cash boost tenants have generated as Palace strove to meet Taylor's all-seater demands. A Whitehorse Lane Stand, with 2,110 seats, was erected during the summer of 1993, two layers of executive boxes replacing 3,000 standing spaces. In May of 1994 the Holmesdale Terrace (11,600 standing) was demolished to make way for a two-tier all-seater (8,600) stand, scheduled for completion in 1995.

Selhurst was opened by the Lord Mayor of London on 30 August 1924, following two and a half years of work transforming it from its usage as a brickfield. Archibald Leitch's design was honoured when, on 1 March 1926, the ground hosted an England v Wales international.

Ground improvements coincided with Palace's rise through the divisions in the 1960s and in 1969 — the year the club rose into the top flight for the

first time — the new Arthur Wait Stand was completed. £2 million was brought into the club in 1983 when Sainsbury's built a new supermarket behind terracing at the Whitehorse Lane End.

Few clubs have closer links with their past ground than Crystal Palace. The name of the club itself stems from its first home — the Sydenham site which was used to rehouse the impressive glass and metal structure built by Joseph Paxton for the Great Exhibition in Hyde Park in 1851.

At the turn of the century the original Crystal Palace was the nation's leading sporting facility — the football arena was used as the venue for the FA Cup Final from 1895 until 1914 and a rugby international was also held there. The new stadium at Crystal Palace is now a leading athletics venue.

Opposite: A bird's-eye view of Selhurst Park in 1949, when Palace languished in Division Three South.

Opposite top: Building for Premiership football in 1994.

Above: The Whitehorse Lane Stand with its two levels of executive boxes emphasised the club's ambition in 1993.

Below: The same view towards Whitehorse Lane when terracing prevailed.

Derby County

CAPACITY:

23,000

HIGHEST ATTENDANCE:

**41,826 v Tottenham Hotspur,
20 September 1969,
Division One**

CAPACITY 1971:

40,500

Between 1991 and 1993 Derby County spent more than £1 million on improvements at the Baseball Ground, their home since 1895. At the same time, however, they decided their future lay elsewhere — specifically, in a proposed new £15 million stadium at Chaddesden Sidings. If given the go-ahead, Derby hope to be in the new stadium for the start of the 1995-96 season.

Derby purchased the Baseball Ground for £10,000 in 1924 from Francis Ley, a local industrialist who introduced baseball to Britain in 1889, and in doing so the club rejected a proposed move to a municipal sports stadium on Osmaston Park Road. Redevelopment culminated in the opening of the 3,300-seater Main Stand in 1926, with the dressing rooms relocated from behind one of the goals, and an increased capacity of 30,000.

The years before World War 2 saw major changes at the Baseball Ground as Derby improved the roof on the Popular Side, built a double-decker stand at the Osmaston End and erected

gypsies to lift a supposed curse prior to the Rams' victorious 1946 Cup Final.

1969 saw Derby celebrating promotion to Division One and the building of a new stand over the East Side terracing. Erected at a cost of £250,000, it incorporated standing room below seats and was named the Ley Stand, resulting in the Baseball Ground becoming one of only four League grounds (with White Hart Lane, Old Trafford and Goodison Park) to have both seats and standing room on all four sides.

In the mid-1970s, the pitch was dug up and a new sand-based surface relaid, with pieces of the old turf sold as souvenirs; more seats were put into the paddock below the Main Stand, the middle tier of the Normanton End and the Osmaston End paddock with the ultimate aim of an all-seater stadium. Unfortunately, crowd segregation necessitated the erecting of fencing around the ground and seats in the Osmaston End were removed in 1983 following violence between rival supporters.

Safety measures in the wake of the Valley Parade fire resulted in the removal of seats to widen gangways, and the dismantling of fences in front of the Main Stand and Normanton End, where a family enclosure, the Key Club, was introduced. By 1993, 15,000 of their 23,000 capacity was seating.

The club's £1 million spending spree between 1991 and 1993 included 33 executive boxes, two restaurants and a specially designed facility for up to 80 disabled fans.

another stand at the Normanton End. The Osmaston Stand suffered bomb damage in January 1941 and after the hostilities ceased there was further talk of the Rams moving to the Municipal Sports Ground though they again decided to stay put. The ground is reported to have been built on the site of an old gypsy camp and Derby persuaded local

Opposite: The pre-development Baseball Ground in 1921, three years before the club bought the ground from industrialist and baseball fan Francis Ley.

Top: By 1993, the view was somewhat more impressive.

Above left: Looking across the ground to the Osmaston End in 1992 and (Left) 1948.

$\mathbb{E}$verton

Everton's arrival at Goodison Park in 1892 was precipitated by a sudden departure from their previous home — at Anfield. The ground that has since become synonymous with their fiercest rivals Liverpool was Everton's home for some eight years, and was even the base when the club won their first League Championship in 1890-91. They left after the rent was more than doubled by the ground's owner John Houlding MP. Following that move Liverpool were formed and the city's footballing rivalry began. Everton left behind a top ground that had already hosted international football and set about establishing themselves at the new site a few hundred yards away.

Three stands, one covered, were erected in time for the visit of Bolton on 2 September 1892. Such was the standard of the ground that it hosted the Notts County v Bolton FA Cup Final two years later and the England v Ireland international in 1889.

The Park End Stand was built in 1907, while the Main Stand was erected and terracing concreted and improved two years later. In 1926 a double-decker stand replaced the wooden 1895 structure that had stood on the Bullens Road side. The building of the new stand on the Gwladys Street end in 1938 was greeted by the visit of King George VI, whose father King George V had been the first monarch to visit a League ground when he visited Goodison in 1913.

Bomb damage from World War 2, during which the ground was used for

CAPACITY:

38,500

HIGHEST ATTENDANCE:

**78,299 v Liverpool,
18 September 1948,
Division One**

CAPACITY 1971:

60,000

training by the Territorial Army, was repaired with compensation from the War Damages Commission, and the entrance from Stanley Park was built in preparation for the 1966 World Cup. Goodison Park hosted three matches from a group comprising Brazil, Portugal, Hungary and Bulgaria, plus the astonishing quarter-final when Portugal beat South Korea 5-3 and the West Germany v USSR semi-final.

The ground has continued to be used for showpiece matches, although its omission from the list of venues chosen for the European Championships in 1996 is a bitter blow — especially as one of the choices is Anfield, the ground Everton left behind in 1892.

Few problems were encountered in complying with the Taylor Report; by 1993 36,500 of Goodison's 38,500 capacity were already seated thanks to the previous year's rebuilding and covering of the Gwladys Street home terrace. A highly impressive £1 million triple-tiered Main Stand had been built in 1971, while a £1.3 million Football Trust grant in 1993 helped development of a new stand at the Park End where visiting supporters were situated. This made Goodison Park an all-seater venue.

Opposite: Substantially covered and, by 1994, completely seated, the Goodison Park of the 1990s was one of the Premiership's most impressive grounds.

Opposite below: The three-tiered Main Stand, built in 1971.

Above: Floodlights were moved to the top of the Bullens Road Stand after completion of the Main Stand.

Bottom: Pictured in May 1950, the Goodison pitch shows understandable signs of wear, while the ground itself has more terracing.

$\mathbb{E}$xeter City

CAPACITY:

10,790

HIGHEST ATTENDANCE:

20,984 v Sunderland,
4 March 1931,
FA Cup 6th Round replay

CAPACITY 1971:

18,500

The proposals for a new stand at the Old Tiverton Road End (3,800 seats to be completed by August 1995) will be the first major development at Exeter's St James' Park for a number of years. While safety work and improved terracing in the 1980s maintained a healthy capacity, Exeter's side stands both date back to the 1920s.

Originally of wooden construction, the Cowshed terrace on the east side of the ground first went up in 1925 although it was not extended to its full length (the cover runs from one six-yard box to the other) until six years later. It has since been re-roofed and the wooden terracing replaced by concrete.

The Main Stand was built in the summer of 1926, a few months after the original stand had been destroyed by fire. The Big Bank at the Old Tiverton Road End — the wide sweep of terracing used by home supporters — was formerly known as the Duke Bank. This was in recognition of H. E. Duke, the local MP, who in 1911 was successful in persuading a neighbouring landowner to sell the club the land which allowed them to extend their pitch to within FA specifications.

During World War 2 the ground was used as a billet and training base for American soldiers.

Pictured three decades apart in 1963 (Top) and 1993, St James' Park Exeter still has little in common with its north-eastern namesake. The Big Bank, to the top of the later picture, will shortly become a stand.

ST JAMES' PARK

Fulham

CAPACITY:

10,400

HIGHEST ATTENDANCE:

49,335 v Millwall,
8 October 1938,
Division Two

CAPACITY 1971:

45,000

Charming though not unique for its riverside location, Craven Cottage (where Fulham FC have played since 1896) is noteworthy as much as for what was nearly done to it as its current form.

The Stevenage Road Stand was erected in 1905 and designed by that doyen of architects, Archibald Leitch. While its old-fashioned wooden construction makes it a candidate for replacement, it has listed building status due to its architectural origin: the gable containing Fulham's name is a prime recognition point. Most famous landmark of all though is the Cottage itself, which contains the club offices and changing rooms and is situated between the Stevenage Road Stand and the uncovered Putney End where visiting supporters gather.

The home Hammersmith End was covered in 1965, while the most recent addition to the Cottage facilities is the Eric Miller Stand, named after the

businessman and sometime board member who proposed its erection in 1972 and who shot himself when the authorities began investigating his business. The stand replaced a Thames-side terrace which offered a round-the-ground route (before segregation was introduced) and thereby prevented spectators from watching the University boat race from the topmost steps, but it has rarely been filled as Fulham, last in the top flight in 1968, sank ever lower in the football firmament.

The ground's future, and that of the club itself, has been under threat since the mid-1980s, when the then chairman Ernie Clay bought the ground freehold from the Church Commissioners. He went on to sell the club and ground to the SB Property Company (Marler

Estates) in 1986. The plan was first to move Fulham to Loftus Road in a merger with QPR, then to cause them to share with Chelsea (whose ground Marler — later Cabra — also owned), enabling Craven Cottage to be developed residentially.

The club, like Chelsea, negotiated an option to buy from the bankers when Cabra went into liquidation — but if purchase is indeed possible, the money will then have to be found to maintain one of the League's most picturesque grounds in the appropriate manner.

Craven Cottage viewed in 1906 (Top) and the late 1980s, in both cases from the Putney End. The Riverside Terrace was replaced in the 1970s by the Eric Miller Stand, to the left of the lower shot.

Grimsby Town

Blundell Park's most dominant feature is the 4,000-seater Findus Stand, so it is fitting that the structure — sponsored by the local frozen fish company — should look out across the Humber Estuary. Built in 1982 at a cost of over £400,000, and incorporating executive boxes, restaurant and offices, the stand replaced the old Barrett Stand. Different coloured seating was used to spell out the name of the stand's sponsor. Seats were also added to the Main Stand paddock at this time.

The deadline to become all-seater by August 1994 prompted the club to add a further 3,000 seats in the remaining standing areas in the Osmond Stand, the Pontoon Stand and the area in front of the Findus Stand.

Two stands from the club's previous Abbey Park home were originally used when Grimsby moved to Blundell Park (actually situated in Cleethorpes, not Grimsby) in 1899. A new Main Stand went up two years later, parts of which still remain today. The Barrett Stand was opened in 1925 and at the end of that decade the Main Stand was extended. The Osmond Stand was erected in 1939, just before the outbreak of World War 2 (Grimsby shared with Scunthorpe at the Old Showground from 1940-44). In 1985-86

the Pontoon Stand (built in 1961), the traditional end for home fans, controversially became the 'away' end at the request of police. It was restored to the home supporters after two years.

CAPACITY:

7,996

HIGHEST ATTENDANCE:

**31,651 v Wolverhampton Wanderers,
20 February 1937,
FA Cup 5th Round**

CAPACITY 1971:

28,000

Above: Blundell Park in 1975, showing the Barrett Stand (left) and Pontoon Stand.

Left: An aerial view in the 1990s shows the Findus Stand (nearest camera), built in 1982 which replaced the Barrett Stand and is still the most modern part of the ground.

Hartlepool United

CAPACITY:

6,721

HIGHEST ATTENDANCE:

17,426 v Manchester Utd,
5 January 1957,
FA Cup 5th Round

CAPACITY 1971:

19,500

Hartlepool's Victoria Ground is permanently assured of its place in the history books as the only ground in the country to have been bombed by Zeppelins during World War 1. Two of the bombs landed on the wooden grandstand, prompting the club to seek compensation of £2,500 from the German government once the war was over — the money never arrived!

The grandstand was finally finished by the events of Bradford in 1985; compulsory designation rendered the Main Stand unusable and so hastened its demolition. Plans are afoot to construct a new Main Stand as and when funding is available. It even has a name — the Cyril Knowles Stand, in memory of the former Tottenham and England player who, as manager of Hartlepool, was instrumental in getting the club promoted to the then Third Division in 1991. But, given the crowds that normally attend the Victoria Ground, finding the funding for this stand is proving to be something of a problem. Therefore the ground is effectively down to three sides.

Over the other side lies the Mill House Stand, an impressive cantilever stand containing 1,600 seats and more than adequate cover for the size of crowd usually found at Hartlepool.

The northeast of England has always been a hotbed of football, able to support three top-class clubs in Newcastle, Sunderland and Middlesbrough. It would be nice to think it could also support one of the perennial strugglers in Hartlepool – and that the Cyril Knowles Stand will one day be built.

The Victoria Ground, Hartlepool, pictured in 1967 (Above) and 1993 (Left). The demolition of the Main Stand in the post-Bradford era is the sad, striking difference, although the Rink End for home supporters has now been covered.

Huddersfield Town

Huddersfield Town's new stadium at Kirklees is proof that the future of sports grounds, in part at least, has already arrived.

The 25,000-seater stadium is a £14 million joint venture between the football club, the Rugby League club and Kirklees Metropolitan Council, who contributed £2 million (and granted the all-important planning permission) on the basis that community facilities would be provided and that the old ground was made available for development. The Football Trust gave £1.5 million towards the scheme.

Facilities on the 51-acre site include a 500-seater banqueting hall, shops and offices, a 24-lane bowling alley, 22 executive boxes, a golf driving range, museums, a health club, a crêche, bar and restaurants. The new stadium is elliptical in shape, with the roofs suspended by futuristic banana-shaped trusses. The stadium will be officially opened in 1995 to coincide with Rugby League's centenary celebrations.

Kirklees Stadium has been built on the banks of the River Colne, close to the famous old Leeds Road ground with which the history of Huddersfield Town is entwined. A series of events, such as guided tours, corporate matches and memorabilia auctions were lined up by the club to mark the 'End of an Era' at Leeds Road.

LEEDS ROAD/KIRKLEES STADIUM

CAPACITY:

25,000

HIGHEST ATTENDANCE:

67,037 v Arsenal,
27 February 1932 (Leeds Road),
FA Cup 6th Round

CAPACITY 1971:

52,000 (Leeds Road)

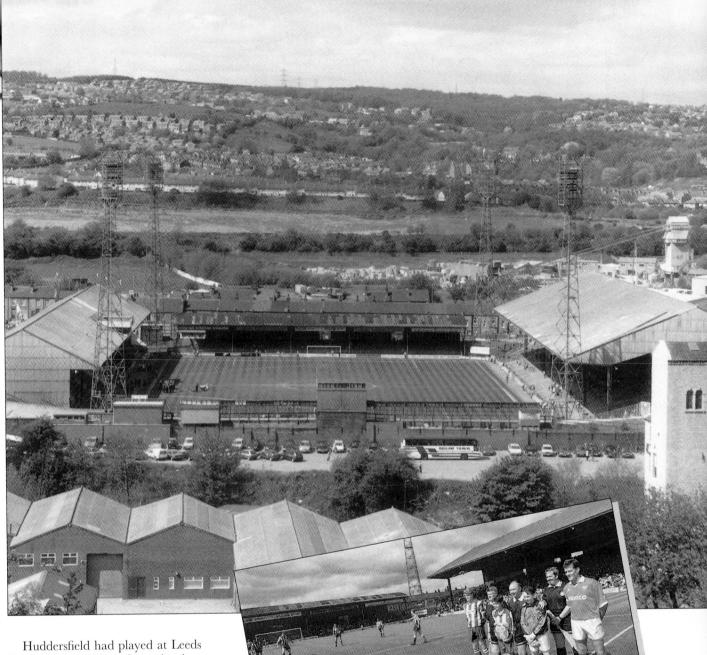

Huddersfield had played at Leeds Road ever since their formation in 1908, one of the most famous days coming on 12 April 1926 when they beat Bolton 3-0 to become the first side to win three League Championships in consecutive seasons. The team had been moulded by the legendary Herbert Chapman, who had moved to Arsenal by the time the club had won the third title.

Over 32,000 watched England beat Holland 8-2 in a full international at Leeds Road on 27 November 1946. The ground also hosted amateur internationals, an international trial, a Northern Rugby League Championship final, plus six FA Cup semi-finals (five

of them in the 1930s). Coincidentally, the first FA Cup semi-final held in Huddersfield in 1882 (Blackburn Rovers v Sheffield Wednesday) was at the St John's rugby ground of Fartown, the club who will share the Kirklees stadium with Huddersfield Town.

Opposite top: Leeds Road, Huddersfield's long-time home, as it was in 1949, three years after it hosted an England international.

Opposite below: Kirklees Stadium under construction, with Leeds Road top left.

Top: A final view of Leeds Road in 1994, where the last game took place in April against Blackpool (Above).

63

Ipswich Town

PORTMAN ROAD

CAPACITY:

22,500

HIGHEST ATTENDANCE:

**38,010 v Leeds United,
8 March 1975,
FA Cup 6th Round**

CAPACITY 1971:

31,500

Ipswich were one of the first clubs in the country to implement the Taylor Report. Their Portman Road ground had become all-seater in the summer of 1992 — the first such stadium in the newly-formed FA Premier League.

Such a forward-looking philosophy should come as no surprise: since the club adopted the ground in 1888, Portman Road has housed sports as diverse as rugby, cricket, whippet racing and American Football.

Largely undeveloped in its formative years, a stand was built and the new pitch inaugurated in 1907, though the stand's roof blew off in a gale four years later. The ground was commandeered by the army during World War 1 for training and storage: they not only ruined the pitch but refused to leave until 1920.

As Arsenal opened their new stand, Ipswich installed 650 of Highbury's unwanted tip-up seats in their Grandstand and proceeded to construct Churchman's Stand. In 1938, Town were elected to the League, more terracing was laid and the two stands extended.

In 1952, the West Side was laid with concrete terracing, having previously seen wooden 'bleachers' since the previous century, and two years later the covered North End was re-terraced.

Work began on a West Stand in 1957, during the Alf Ramsey era, a two-tier structure with pitched roof for which plans had first been announced three years earlier (team building took priority at the supporters' request); the North Stand terracing was improved,

with the pavilion being replaced by offices and dressing rooms in 1965.

Ipswich enjoyed a period of success under Bobby Robson in the 1970s, during which the East Stand was dismantled and the Portman Road Stand, encompassing 3,700 seats, was erected. Over the years, wings have been added with a restaurant, club shop and squash court built underneath.

A sum of £300,000 saw the Churchman's Stand rebuilt in 1977, while their FA Cup Final success over Arsenal the following year enabled funds to be made available to install 1,800 seats and 24 executive boxes in the Portman Road Stand.

Following safety improvements necessary with the introduction of the Safety of Sports Grounds Act, the Pioneer Stand was built over the existing West Stand at a cost of £1.4 million in 1982; 4,800 seats

were added after the dismantling of the old roof, bringing the capacity to 37,000.

In 1993, a new stadium control box was built at a cost of £100,000 which brought a police surveillance unit, PA announcer, scoreboard operator and emergency services under the same roof for the first time. The old police box, situated on the Pioneer Terrace, made way for 450 extra seats.

Opposite: Portman Road as seen from the air in 1935, three years before they gained League status and subsequent development.

Top: The ground in 1993, 12 months after it had become all-seater.

Above: Thirty years earlier, the East Anglian public could choose to watch from the terrace or the stand.

Leeds United

CAPACITY:

40,000

HIGHEST ATTENDANCE:

**57,892 v Sunderland,
15 March 1967,
FA Cup 5th Round replay**

CAPACITY 1971:

50,500

Elland Road (then known as the Old Peacocks Ground) was bought by Holbeck Rugby Club in 1897. Football was first played there a year later when it hosted the West Yorkshire Cup Final between Hunslet and Harrogate, but the ground did not become home to Leeds City until 1904. Hull City were the first visitors for a friendly match on 15 October.

The FA ruled that City should be disbanded in 1919 (their manager at the time was Herbert Chapman) following allegations of illegal payments made to players and, after hosting a

handful of Yorkshire Amateurs' games, Elland Road became home to the newly formed Leeds United. When the club reached the First Division in 1924 Elland Road had a Main Stand on the west side, a covered terrace at the Elland Road End, a long stand on the Lowfields Road side and open terracing at the North (Kop) End.

Huddersfield Town played two games at Elland Road in 1950 following a fire in their Main Stand and, ironically, just six years later, on 18 September 1956, the Main Stand at Leeds suffered the same fate. It caused

£100,000 worth of damage and destroyed offices, dressing rooms, directors' rooms, even the playing kit and equipment. The new 10,000-capacity (4,000 seats) West Stand was opened for the game with Leicester on 31 August 1957.

Like so many clubs it was the arrival of one man, in this case Don Revie in 1961, that was to transform the ground by bringing success on the pitch. He took Leeds from the Second Division to one of the leading club sides in Europe and profits from the success were ploughed back into the ground. In 1968 the open Kop was replaced by a covered terraced stand, a development which resulted in the pitch being shifted 30ft so that one goal stood where the base of the old terracing had lain. A corner section, with seating at the back, joined the North and West Stands in 1970 and the north east corner was erected a year later. The pitch was again moved northwards in 1974 when the 7,500-capacity (3,500 seats) South Stand was built at a cost of £500,000.

In 1985 Elland Road hosted an England v New Zealand Rugby League Test match. The same year Bradford City played three home matches at Leeds following the fire at Valley Parade. The FA Vase Final replay between Bridlington and Yeading was also held at Elland Road in 1990. The ground has been chosen as a venue for the European Championships in 1996.

In the 1989-90 season a family stand (2,800-capacity) and boxes were built at a cost of £500,000. The south east corner was constructed in the summer of 1991 for £820,000 (1,300 seats) and the £1.3 million banqueting suite followed that same season. The Lowfields Road Stand was demolished in 1992 to make way for a 17,000 all-seater two-tiered East Stand, costing £6.5 million and boasting the largest cantilever roof span of any ground in Europe. The North Stand (Kop) was seated in the summer of 1994 at a cost of £1.1 million, adding a further 6,800 seats.

Opposite: Elland Road in 1962, with the open South Terrace clearly visible.

Inset opposite: The public face of Leeds in Don Revie's 1970s era of success.

Top: Looking towards the North Stand (Kop) in 1978.

Above left: The new East Stand, unveiled in mid 1993, boasts the largest cantilever roof in any European ground.

Left: 1967 action in front of the West Stand.

Leicester City

CAPACITY:

23,000

HIGHEST ATTENDANCE:

47,298 v Tottenham Hotspur,
18 February 1928,
FA Cup 5th Round

CAPACITY 1971:

42,000

Leicester Fosse (as they were known until 1919) moved into Filbert Street in 1891, having had six grounds in the previous 17 years. Archibald Leitch was a major influence on the ground's early development before World War 1.

The Main Stand was opened in 1921, with the South Stand being built in the summer of 1927, and at the time Leicester played host to their record attendance in 1928 both the Popular Side and the North Terrace were being covered. Wartime damage to the Main Stand was not completely repaired until 1949.

Following promotion to the top flight in 1971, the North Stand and East Side saw seats being installed, and in 1975 the North Stand roof was replaced by 20 private boxes.

Being another ground to suffer from insufficient ventilation, the Filbert Street playing surface tended to be muddy during the winter months. Leicester attempted to combat this by installing a huge plastic sheet over the pitch which could be raised by hot air — high enough for players to train underneath. Unfortunately, the cost of running this was high and as drainage was improved the cover was dispensed with.

The option to relocate out of town to a new site near the M1 motorway was considered after the Taylor Report, as was the plan to turn the pitch through 90 degrees. They could not get planning permission for the latter, so the pitch stayed the same and the Main Stand changed instead at a cost of £5.35 million (£1.8 million from the Football Trust). It holds nearly 9,500, but the old double-decker stand behind

the goal at the south end of Filbert Street still provided the best view.

The East Stand, opposite the new Main Stand, is small but adequate and the North Stand boasts the Captain's

Club — Leicester's restaurant open during the week as well as on matchdays. In 1994, the Kop was made all-seater to comply with Taylor, losing 1,000 from the maximum capacity in the process.

As chairman Martin George announced, Filbert Street was now not merely a football ground but 'a multi-purpose operation boasting the best in conference, banqueting and corporate hospitality facilities'.

Opposite: Leicester's imposing Main Stand is responsible for 9,500 of the ground's 23,000 capacity.

Above: A view across Filbert Street from north to south, taken in 1947.

Above left: The South End again, this time in 1978 with the former Main Stand visible alongside.

Left: Executive boxes at the North End overlook this 1979 action.

Leyton Orient

the proposed 16,000-seater stadium, with sports hall, restaurant, new offices, shop and executive seating, would begin at the end of the 1995-96 season. The cost is estimated at £8 million.

Brisbane Road, officially the Leyton Stadium, has been home to Orient since 1937, when they took over from Leyton Amateurs. At that stage, there was one stand on the west side and no concrete terracing. The Main Stand went up in 1956 and had been extended by the time the club entered the top flight in 1962. The terracing on the east was also improved and increased. Seats were added to the West Terrace in 1977.

In the late 1980s the club had planned to groundshare with West Ham at a new purpose-built stadium at Lee Valley Regional Park. In the event, West Ham decided to redevelop their own Upton Park instead, paving the way for Orient's 1994 plans.

Let nobody accuse Leyton Orient of being afraid of change at their Brisbane Road ground. In March 1994 the club unveiled a scheme, drawn up by architect and club director John Goldsmith, to rotate the pitch through 90 degrees. Although hemmed in on all sides by roads, the club announced that they had been in negotiations with planners to extend the ground into Oliver Road and the tennis courts behind, rerouting the road in the process. If the club is successful in gaining planning permission work on

Top: This view of Brisbane Road in 1975 shows the north and south terraces behind the goals. Current plans are to rotate the pitch through 90 degrees.

Above: The groundsman applies the roller in 1993, as Main Stand spectators look on.

CAPACITY:

17,000

HIGHEST ATTENDANCE:

34,345 v West Ham Utd,
25 January 1964,
FA Cup 4th Round

CAPACITY 1971:

35,000

Lincoln City

Fourth Division basement could not afford such grandiose plans, and by leaving out the executive boxes and 400 of the seats, the bill came down to a slightly more manageable £300,000.

Ironically, Lincoln's fortunes picked up when least expected: two consecutive seasons of relegation saw them become the first club to be automatically demoted into the Vauxhall Conference. The decision to remain full-time paid dividends, for not only did the club win promotion in 1988 but crowds were considerably up in the process.

CAPACITY:

12,461

HIGHEST ATTENDANCE:

**23,196 v Derby County,
15 November 1967,
League Cup 4th Round**

CAPACITY 1971:

25,300

Lincoln City have been resident at Sincil Bank since 1894 when the club moved from their John O'Gaunts ground. At first the ground was simple in design, a small wooden grandstand being built and supporters helping to build the earth banks. A second, similar stand was constructed at the south end and, as the South Park Stand, housed the offices and dressing rooms until it burnt down in 1924. Although a replacement was built, the offices and dressing rooms were relocated in the Main Stand, also known as St Andrew's Stand, just after World War One.

Lincoln's role as perennial strugglers on the pitch was coupled with constant problems off it, culminating in the decision to sell the ground to the local council and take out a 21-year lease at £1,000 a year in 1982, with a buy-back option in three years. Lincoln were never in a position to exercise that option, for the Bradford fire (when Lincoln were the visitors) in 1985 and resultant legislation meant the removal of part of the Railway End terrace roof and the subsequent demolition of the Main Stand, greatly reducing the capacity with a resultant loss of income. Plans were laid to construct a new Main Stand at a cost of £750,000, complete with executive boxes and 1,400 seats. A club struggling in the

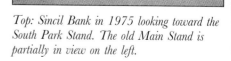

Top: Sincil Bank in 1975 looking toward the South Park Stand. The old Main Stand is partially in view on the left.

Middle: The addition of seats behind the goal created the Stacey West Stand.

Above: Though scaled down, the new 1,000-seat Main Stand is undoubtedly impressive.

L*iverpool*

CAPACITY:

40,000

HIGHEST ATTENDANCE:

61,905 v Wolverhampton
Wanderers,
2 February 1952,
FA Cup 4th Round

CAPACITY 1971:

54,945

The redevelopment of the Kop at Anfield in the summer of 1994 signalled the end of an era in British football grounds. Although there are many Kops across the country, the term has always been most closely associated with Anfield. Liverpool have traditionally claimed to have the first Kop (although there is evidence from Arsenal that may dispute this) and the Kop's supporters are renowned for their fervent, yet sporting, support. So it was symbolic of the changes to grounds throughout the country when the Spion Kop was converted into a 12,400 all-seater stand. Chunks of the famous terrace were sold off to raise money for the Liverpool University Hospital.

Anfield has proved a daunting battleground for visiting teams since the 1960s, but off the pitch the supporters of those teams have more reason to be cheerful. Anfield, named as one of the eight venues to be used during the 1996 European Championships, is one of the nation's top grounds.

Previously used by rivals

Everton, Anfield became home for the newly-formed red side of the city when Everton fell into dispute with the landlord over rent in 1892. Liverpool were as close to a ready-packaged club as you could get. Professional players, limited company and a ground of First Division standard from the very beginning, it took them just a year before they were elected to the Second Division and nine years before they had the First Division title in their grasp.

The first Main Stand went up in 1895 and its distinctive Tudor-style gable, displaying the name of the club, stood guard over Anfield's pitch until the 1970s. The Anfield Road End got its first stand in 1903, the famous Kop banking (named after the Spion Kop in South Africa, where many Merseyside soldiers perished in the Boer War) emerging three years later.

King George V and Queen Mary visited Anfield in 1921 to see Wolves defeat Cardiff in an FA Cup semi-final replay, and in 1928 the Kop was covered and extended to hold just under 30,000.

The arrival of Bill Shankly, the club's legendary manager, in 1959 signalled big changes at Anfield. As he laid the foundations for a club that was to dominate domestic and European football for years to come, so Liverpool upgraded their ground to mirror the on-field success.

In 1963, a year after the club gained promotion to the top flight (they have been there ever since), the Kemlyn Road Stand was pulled down and

Opposite top: The view across Anfield towards the Centenary Stand in 1993, with the Anfield Road Stand away to the left.

Opposite bottom: The famous Shankly Gate.

Top: Programme for the Kop's swansong, on 30 April 1994 against Norwich City.

Above and left: Two views of the Kop in its final months as Britain's most famous terrace.

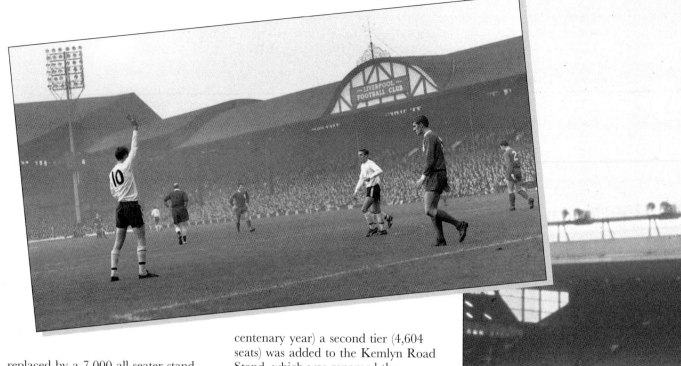

replaced by a 7,000 all-seater stand. Ten years later a new Main Stand was officially opened by HRH The Duke of Kent and a new floodlighting system installed.

Bill Shankly, who died in 1981, had taken Liverpool from a Second Division outfit in the 1960s to a club that was to become the best in Europe by the end of the next decade: fittingly, the Shankly Gate at the Anfield Road entrance to the car park behind the Main Stand was named in his honour. Across the top of the ornate iron gates read the words: 'You'll Never Walk Alone'. To the left of these gates a plaque has been erected to commemorate those supporters who lost their lives at Hillsborough in 1989.

A new entrance and ticket office, which projected from the Main Stand on to the car park, was opened in August 1979. During the next close season an underpitch heating system was laid and the paddock terrace in the Main Stand converted into an all-seater area (capacity 2,350), which meant raising part of the terracing. In May 1982 work began on adding 4,000 seats to the terraced Anfield Road End, which gave the ground a capacity of 45,000 (21,850 seats).

In the summer of 1992 (the club's

centenary year) a second tier (4,604 seats) was added to the Kemlyn Road Stand, which was renamed the Centenary Stand. A car park replaced the row of houses which had to be demolished to make way for the development. The club offices are also located on this side of the ground.

Anfield's international history started as far back as 1883, when Everton were still tenants, with England beating Ireland 7-0. In more recent times, the ground will be remembered as host for the crucial Wales v Scotland World Cup qualifier in 1977. Kenny Dalglish, who had arrived at Liverpool only months earlier as replacement for the Hamburg-bound Kevin Keegan, scored for Scotland in a 2-0 win. And despite the Kop's redevelopment and Liverpool's eclipse by Manchester United in the 1990s as the nation's dominant team, there were clearly more great spectacles ahead.

Top: Fulham's Johnny Haynes salutes the Main Stand in 1966. Both player and Stand 'retired' not long afterwards, the latter to be replaced in the early 1970s by today's imposing edifice.

Right: The Main Stand pictured in the late 1970s, just before its paddock area was seated. This added just over 2,000 to its existing upper-section capacity of 8,600.

74

Luton Town

CAPACITY:

13,449

HIGHEST ATTENDANCE:

**30,069 v Blackpool,
4 March 1959,
FA Cup 6th Round replay**

CAPACITY 1971:

31,000

Even by the standards of 1905, when the ground first opened, Kenilworth Road was not the ideal location for a football ground, hemmed in by a railway on one side and houses on two. In the 1990s, the situation is considerably worse: add the traffic generated by a football crowd and you have an area of the town that comes to a complete standstill every other Saturday afternoon.

While the current capacity of nearly 13,500 is hardly ideal, the present ground is little more than a short-term solution to Luton's problems. The Main Stand was built in the 1920s to replace an existing stand which burnt down, with the centre section of the new structure purchased from the Kempton racetrack. On the opposite side is the

Bobbers Stand, so-named because when it was built in 1933 it cost a shilling (or a bob) to stand there. While this was originally built as terracing, it became all-seater in 1977 and then, towards the end of 1986, was altered once again to contain private executive boxes.

This is perhaps the only ground in the country where executive boxes form an entire side of the stadium; they are styled on Lord's Cricket Ground, with guests in the box able to finish their meal, slide open the glass doors and take their seats on a private balcony to watch the action.

The former visitors' terrace, at the Kenilworth Road End, was covered at much the same time as the ground became members-only. The entrance to the stand was as forbidding as any

Opposite: Kenilworth Road's Bobbers Stand in 1985, shortly before its conversion to executive boxes.

Left: This aerial view, taken in 1927, graphically illustrates Luton's lack of room for development.

Below left: Luton entertain Sheffield Wednesday on their synthetic pitch in March 1986 even though the terracing is inhospitably snow-covered.

Bottom: Action on grass in the early 1970s, with the proximity of neighbouring houses graphically illustrated.

are allowed back at the ground. The stand itself is accessed by a route that can only be described as through four back gardens and up a fire escape, but it is perhaps this stand which encapsulates Luton's problems — there is no room whatsoever to enlarge the ground.

A relief road has been built, thereby cutting the Main Stand even further. If, as has been threatened, the FA decide to introduce rules governing stadia for clubs in the Premier Division, Kenilworth Road is very unlikely to play host to the likes of Manchester United in the battle for Premiership points.

For all of the animosity Luton generated in the 1980s by the laying of an artificial pitch and the members-only policy, Kenilworth Road is a homely ground. Manchester United and Old Trafford may well be a vision of football's future, but Luton Town and Kenilworth Road are a pleasant reminder of its friendly past.

prison, with eight-foot high fences and giant turnstiles, which would operate only with the correct credit card-style ticket. Now the Kenilworth Road End is all-seater and the capacity of this end, 8,000 when it was all-standing, greatly reduced.

At the opposite end is the Oak Road End which has a unique and unusual roof built in three sections. This stand has also been converted to all-seating, and accommodates visitors now they

Manchester City

MAINE ROAD

CAPACITY:

21,500 (pending redevelopment of Kippax Stand)

HIGHEST ATTENDANCE:

**84,569 v Stoke City,
3 March 1934,
FA Cup 6th Round**

CAPACITY 1971:

64,374

The successful bid to take over Manchester City in February 1994 by a group headed by former player Francis Lee threw plans for the completion of Maine Road's redevelopment into confusion. A new 10,000-seater Kippax Stand had been scheduled to be built in the summer of 1994 in order to meet the Taylor Report's all-seater deadline. The new owners were not happy with the plans, however, and sought an FA extension while they drew up alternative plans. A larger, more ambitious project that will enhance Maine Road's standing as a big-match venue seems likely.

Part of the ground's redevelopment was unveiled in early 1993 with the opening of the new Umbro Stand. Replacing the old Platt Lane Stand, which had been demolished the previous year, the new stand has seats for 4,539 spectators.

Maine Road missed out on selection as a venue for the 1996 European Championships and certainly its use for showpiece games has been affected due to the closeness of Old Trafford and to a lesser extent Liverpool and Sheffield.

The fans did little to enhance Maine Road's reputation on 7 May 1993 — the opening day of the new stand — when, trailing in an FA Cup quarter-final to Tottenham, they invaded the pitch, taking full advantage of perimeter fences being down post-Hillsborough. Referee Ray Lewis, who, with sad irony, had been in charge at Hillsborough, was forced to take the players off the pitch while police restored calm. It helped little that the world's eyes were upon the city at the time because of Manchester's bid to host the Olympics.

Lewis said: 'So soon after Hillsborough, I was very worried that day. I feared the worst and felt that it was possibly going to happen all over again. It certainly raised all the questions about fences again.'

Sixty fans were banned from Maine Road for life as a result, but it undoubtedly dented Maine Road's future as a big-match venue.

City moved to Maine Road in 1923 from Hyde Road, a ground which had served them for the previous 26 years and had played host to King Edward VII and future Prime Minister Balfour. The one stand (seating 10,000) towered out over the rest of the open, sweeping concrete terracing.

Neighbours United moved into Maine Road for eight years from 1941 because of bomb damage to Old Trafford and a year before they left 82,950 came to see them play Arsenal — higher than the record attendance at their own ground.

On the back of the extra money generated by the tenants, seating was added at the Platt Lane End, floodlights erected and the Kippax Street terracing covered. A new North Stand went up in the 1960s and in 1982 a new roof covered the Main Stand.

Opposite top: Maine Road in 1923, the year Manchester City moved there from nearby Hyde Road. The single 10,000-seater stand is clearly visible.

Opposite below: City's George Heslop and Fulham's Les Barrett battle it out in 1968, with the Kippax in the background.

Left: The Umbro Stand replaced the old Platt Lane Stand in 1993.

Below: Maine Road in 1978.

Manchester United

CAPACITY:

43,500

HIGHEST ATTENDANCE:

**70,504 v Aston Villa,
27 December 1920,
Division One**

CAPACITY 1971:

63,500

As the outstanding English club side of the early 1990s, Manchester United were in the enviable position of having a ground to match. The half-century between Old Trafford's wartime bombing and the all-seater stadium of 1994 had seen many stirring stories on the field — and while the ground's capacity had decreased by around one third over the period, this in no way reflected a lack of demand to see the legendary club in action on home turf.

The Old Trafford story started back in 1909 when local brewer J. H. Davies (who had been responsible for reviving the club after their predecessors, Newton Heath, went into liquidation in 1902) paid the sum of £60,000 to purchase a site a few miles from their previous Clayton ground. Archibald Leitch supervised the construction of a multi-span roofed stand which was opened in February 1910. The late 1920s saw the extension of the multi-span roof and the United Road side standing area covered.

German bombers which raided the nearby Trafford Park industrial estate

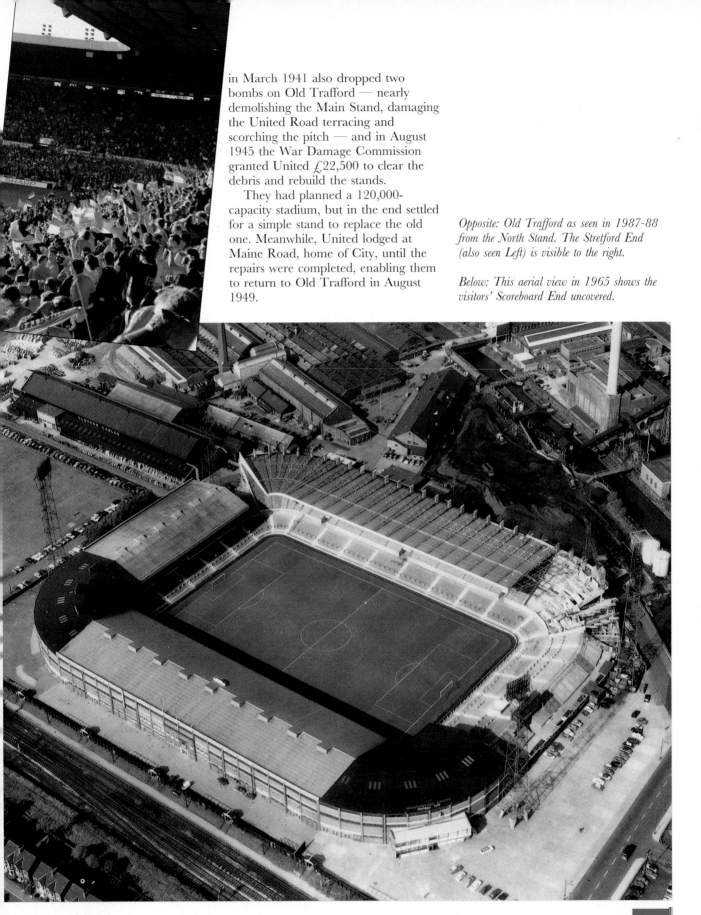

in March 1941 also dropped two
bombs on Old Trafford — nearly
demolishing the Main Stand, damaging
the United Road terracing and
scorching the pitch — and in August
1945 the War Damage Commission
granted United £22,500 to clear the
debris and rebuild the stands.

They had planned a 120,000-
capacity stadium, but in the end settled
for a simple stand to replace the old
one. Meanwhile, United lodged at
Maine Road, home of City, until the
repairs were completed, enabling them
to return to Old Trafford in August
1949.

*Opposite: Old Trafford as seen in 1987-88
from the North Stand. The Stretford End
(also seen Left) is visible to the right.*

*Below: This aerial view in 1965 shows the
visitors' Scoreboard End uncovered.*

The Main Stand remained uncovered until 1951 and the home Stretford End for another eight years. Asked to prepare for the World Cup and presented with a grant for £40,000, United tore down the United Road cover and built an impressive cantilever construction which allowed for expansion at both ends and catered for both seated and standing spectators, as well as including the first executive boxes at a British football ground. All in all, a total of £426,000 was spent improving Old Trafford for the World Cup games, the last section of the ground to remain exposed to the elements being the Scoreboard End.

Work converting every roof to cantilever construction started in 1978 with the Main Stand, continuing until 75% of the ground was covered in this way in August 1985 — only one corner

and the Stretford End then requiring
completion. The following year also saw
the replacement of original floodlight
pylons with lights anchored on gantries
around the roof.

The Manchester United Museum
was incorporated in the mid-1980s, and
was believed to be the first such facility
at any club ground in the world. The
Sir Matt Busby Suite was opened in
May 1986, and included photographs
and plans of United grounds, both past
and present, and a 1958 telegram from
Duncan Edwards to his landlady
informing her that their flight from
Munich had been delayed.

The redevelopment of standing areas
was undertaken over four years in the
early 1990s, the jewel in the crown
being the new totally seated Stretford
End, unveiled at the beginning of the
1993-94 season. This left the only
standing area at the visitors' end behind
the facing goal, and this was finally
seated in 1994. The 'bowl' shape of the
ground was continued around to form a
perfect ellipse, while behind the scenes
a new ground control room and PA
system was installed. Finally,
modernisation of dressing room facilities
led to a highly visible difference: the
resiting of the players' tunnel between
the Main Stand and the Stretford End
and not centrally through the Main
Stand as before.

*Opposite top: Looking over to the newly-seated
Stretford End, opened at the beginning of
1993-94.*

*Opposite below: This 1993 view of Old
Trafford emphasises the cantilever roof that
now forms a perfect ellipse around the ground.*

*Top: The North Stand spells it out – this is
the home of the Premiership Champions.*

Above: Old Trafford from pitch level in 1975.

Middlesbrough

AYRESOME PARK

CAPACITY:
26,000

HIGHEST ATTENDANCE:
**53,596 v Newcastle Utd,
27 December 1949,
Division One**

CAPACITY 1971:
42,000

Middlesbrough's announcement that they are to quit Ayresome Park for a new 32,000-capacity all-seater stadium in 1995 (see Future Grounds) means the sad loss of a stadium with a proud history.

Ayresome Park was once one of the top stadia in the country and in July 1966 it played host to the exciting World Cup exploits of the North Koreans, including their 1-0 win over Italy. Middlesbrough had been chosen only as a late replacement for St James' Park, but the decision prompted the installation of new seats on both sides of the ground plus a new roof and seats for the east end.

Middlesbrough moved to Ayresome Park in 1903, a 40,000-capacity ground with stands on both the north and south sides. The first of three Home Internationals was held there in 1905 (England 1 Ireland 1). The South Stand was rebuilt in 1936 and improvements to the banking behind the goals followed, including a cover for the Holgate End. In 1986, after years of wrangling with council planners, the club finally opened a public sports hall alongside the ground. Just over 2,000 seats were installed on the south terrace in the same year and seating for 4,000 was added to the East End in 1990.

Top: Middlesbrough's South Stand, pictured in 1992 – two years before a decision to quit Ayresome Park was announced.

Left: Ayresome action in 1974, with spectators in the North Stand looking on.

Millwall

CAPACITY:

20,146

HIGHEST ATTENDANCE:

48,672 v Derby,
20 February 1937,
FA Cup 5th Round

CAPACITY 1971:

40,000

Above: As this view suggests, Millwall's new ground in 1993 remained a Den.

Right: The first ever League match to be played on a Sunday in January 1974 took place at its predecessor.

In July 1993 Millwall moved, after 83 years, 400yd from their ground the Den, Cold Blow Lane, to a new stadium.

The New Den is an impressive £15.5 million all-seater stadium situated close to South Bermondsey railway station. The first game at the new ground was a prestigious friendly against Portugal's Sporting Lisbon, led by ex-England manager Bobby Robson, on 4 August 1993 (Millwall lost 2-1). The official opening ceremony was performed by the late Labour leader

John Smith. It was the first new League football ground to be built in London since 1924 and its existence is made all the more remarkable in that when City financier Reg Burr took over as chairman at the club in 1986, the Lions, despite having just gained promotion from the Third Division, were facing liquidation.

Millwall sold their old ground to Fairview New Homes for £5.2 million and were given £2.75 million from the Football Trust, but it was a deal with Lewisham Borough Council which sealed the decision to move. The council contributed £2.7 million towards the new ground, and, more importantly, they handed the club a 125-year lease. Income from rents and sales service the rest of the debt. Money can also be generated from hosting events such as music concerts, Rugby League and boxing. In March 1994, the New Den held the all-British World Heavyweight Boxing title fight between Herbie Hide and Michael Bentt.

It took 57 weeks to transform the previous sports playing field into the four two-tiered stands which comprise the 20,000 all-seater stadium. Spelt out in a sea of mainly blue seats the words 'THE DEN' (in yellow) provide a link with Millwall's past at Cold Blow Lane. The corners of the ground have been left open so as to assist in the drying and ventilation of the pitch — a problem faced by many enclosed stadia.

The New Den includes restaurants, executive lounges, 32 executive boxes and parking for 240 cars on-site and a further 4,500 off-site. There are 56 television monitors for pre-match entertainment — monitors as opposed to screens because 24 of them contain cameras for purposes of crowd control. The dressing rooms include relaxation rooms, weights, benches, even jacuzzis. There are also all-weather pitches, a community hall and a crêche run by the council.

Although houses are the future for Cold Blow Lane, history will remember the site clearly as Millwall's Den. The club's nickname (the Lions) made the Den a likely name for the ground when the club first moved there some 25 years and four previous grounds after their formation.

FA President Lord Kinnaird opened

the ground in 1910 and the following year England beat Wales 3-0 as international football came to the Den.

Bomb damage, largely to the Main Stand, during World War 2 forced Millwall to leave the Den to share with Charlton at the Valley for a time, although reserve matches did continue. Using compensation from the War Damages Commission, Millwall set about restoration and ten years after

the war had ended they had completed the covering around the ground.

League football on a Sunday is now commonplace but it was on 20 January 1974 that the Den hosted the first ever Sunday game when they played Fulham. In 1990 Millwall's promotion to the First Division wiped out the Den's unwanted tag as the only London venue not to have staged top-flight football.

Inset opposite: A sparse crowd sees Millwall play Derby at the Old Den in early 1993.

Above: A full house later that year when the new ground opened with a prestige friendly against Sporting Lisbon.

Left: This shot from the same game shows the 20,000-seater stadium's futuristic stand design.

Newcastle United

Renowned as one of the nation's hotbeds of soccer, Newcastle now has a stadium that matches the aspirations of its fervent supporters. As the northeast's sleeping giant awakened in the late 1980s so did St James' Park.

In 1987 the West Stand, which had been condemned by the local authority as unsafe, was demolished. In its place rose the new £5 million Milburn Stand (named after the club's famous centre-forward Jackie Milburn who died in October 1988). In 1993, as the club moved towards meeting Taylor's all-seater requirements, the Leazes Terrace was demolished and replaced by the Sir John Hall Stand (11,100 seats). In 1994 the Gallowgate Terrace was pulled down to make way for a new 11,000-seater Gallowgate Stand.

St James' Park's selection as a venue for the 1996 European Championships came as just reward for the redeveloped ground and makes partial, if late,

amends to a city which missed out on the World Cup 30 years earlier.

St James' Park had initially been named as a 1966 venue but wrangling with the city planners over a lease left them out in the cold for the big event — a decision made worse for their supporters by the use of their rivals' Roker Park ground in the Finals. Such was the club's anger that they threatened to quit the city altogether — an argument that was not resolved until 1971, when new plans for the ground were approved by the council.

Newcastle Rangers played the first competitive match at St James' Park in November 1880 but it was not until 12 years later that Newcastle East End, the forerunners of United, used the ground for the first time, when they took on Glasgow Celtic in a friendly.

The first West Stand went up in 1897 but it was two years before the ground started taking shape, with a stand at the Gallowgate End and terracing at the Leazes End and the East Bank. Capacity was 30,000. The first of seven St James' Park

CAPACITY:

39,000

HIGHEST ATTENDANCE:

**68,386 v Chelsea,
3 September 1930,
Division One**

CAPACITY 1971:

61,500

internationals followed in 1901 (England 6 Wales 0). A new West Stand and extended terracing almost doubled the capacity just after the turn of the century.

The Leazes End was covered in 1930 but it was not until 1972 that major changes started to occur, when the same end was redeveloped. It was the repair bills that the West Stand was handed following the post-Bradford fire safety inspections that prompted the changes that have shaped the new St James' Park.

Opposite: The East side of St James' Park is pictured as terracing in 1967 (Top left) and in 1993.

Left: The same East Stand late in 1993, now linked with the 11,100-seat Sir John Hall Stand. Opened that year, it replaced the Leazes Terrace.

Above: Back in 1927, only the West Stand (nearest camera) offered seating accommodation.

Northampton Town

CAPACITY:

7,600 (new stadium)

HIGHEST ATTENDANCE:

24,523 v Fulham,
23 April 1966,
Division One

CAPACITY 1971:

21,000

When plans were floated for Northampton Town FC to move in 1994 to a new sports ground built by the borough council and for which the football club would pay a peppercorn rent, it spelled the end of a football-cricket link that had survived for just short of a century.

Although many football clubs owe their very existence to cricket club members looking for a sport to play during the winter months, at only two League grounds did the two sports co-exist — Sheffield United's Bramall Lane and Northampton Town's County Ground. (Although the cricket and football pitches are linked at Darlington's Feethams Ground, the football pitch is enclosed on all four sides.)

While Sheffield United were eventually able to cast aside their cricketing co-habitees (and now boast one of the largest car parks in League football), Northampton Town continued to share their ground with the county cricket side, so only three sides of the ground had been developed.

Although the cricket club had been resident since the 1880s, football did not find its way to the County Ground until 1897, utilising the already existing cricket pavilion but with the proviso that no football was played before 1 September or after 1 May. It was ten years before the football club began building their own facilities, with the terraces and a small stand built between 1907 and 1912 when Herbert

Chapman was manager. Progress on the field (they were admitted to the Football League in 1920) was coupled with progress off it, a Main Stand built in 1924 being damaged by a fire in 1929 but soon restored to its former glories.

In the 1960s Northampton arrived in the First Division, for the first time in their history, in 1965. Sadly, they completed the return journey just as rapidly, but even when the crowds were being drawn by the likes of visitors Arsenal, Liverpool, Tottenham, Manchester United *et al*, the tenants of the cricket club were unable to develop the fourth side of the ground. Once the club were back in the basement there

was little or no need for a greater capacity and the chance to improve the ground was gone, seemingly for ever.

Northampton suffered further with the 1985 designation of sports grounds, resulting in the top half of the Main Stand being removed and the reappearance of temporary stands. Various other sections of the ground have been dismantled or closed off and in 1994 the County Ground 'boasted' a capacity of 8,553. Meanwhile, the need for a larger capacity diminished with each passing week as the club struggled to remain in the Football League and out of the hands of the liquidators.

In 1994, plans for a new ground approached reality with the

announcement of a £4.5 million, 7,600-capacity stadium known as Sixfields, near Duston, £1 million of the funds for which were provided by the Football Ground Improvement Trust.

Opposite top: The County Ground from the air in 1926, showing its proximity to the cricket square.

Opposite: As can be seen here, rudimentary barriers had to be used to create a fourth side to the pitch.

Above: A view of the County Ground in the 1965 close season.

Norwich City

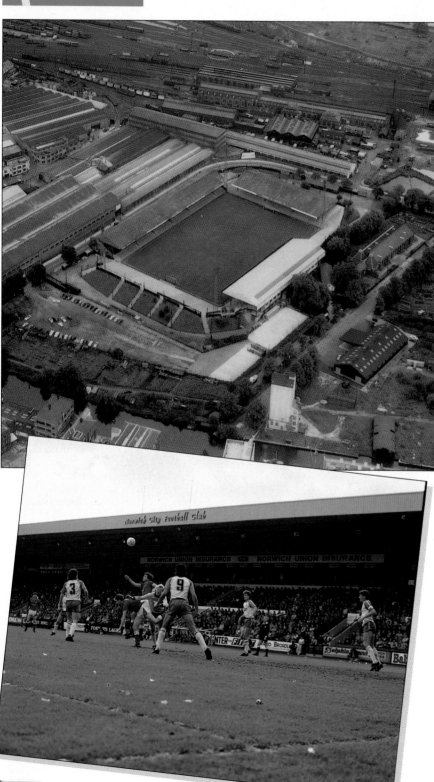

CAPACITY:

21,200

HIGHEST ATTENDANCE:

**43,984 v Leicester City,
30 March 1963,
FA Cup 6th Round**

CAPACITY 1971:

48,000

Carrow Road came of age in the autumn of 1993. A ground born into Second Division football in 1935 was playing host to some of the world's top club sides.

The UEFA Cup visits of Vitesse Arnhem, Bayern Munich and Inter Milan, in Norwich's first European foray, brought top quality continental teams to this neat and modern ground in East Anglia. Such opposition brought near sell-out crowds (16,818, 20,829 and 20,805 respectively) but a comparison with the highest crowd at Carrow Road (43,984) reflects perfectly the shrinking capacities of English grounds.

Norwich City's rise from original members of the Third Division in 1920 (when the club still played at the Nest, Rosary Road) has been steady, if not meteoric. As the veritable 'club with limited resources' the ground has had to develop at City's own pace.

Norwich moved to Carrow Road in 1935, kicking off at their new home against West Ham on 31 August, when there was one stand and three sides of terracing. Three years later on 29 October, King George VI visited Carrow Road to watch the game against Millwall.

Floodlights went up in 1956 and terracing to the south was covered in the mid-1960s, but it was not until the next decade that major change came to Norwich. First the South Stand was

Opposite top: Carrow Road in 1961.

Opposite bottom: Action from Norwich v Everton in 1986-87 with the City Stand in the background.

Left: Norwich's ground in 1993 featured two new additions, the River End (nearest camera) and Barclay Stands.

Bottom: Norwich by night, 1994.

Below: A 1975 goal at the Barclay End.

covered, then, in 1979, at a cost of £1.7 million the River End was replaced with a new stand (a mix of seats and terracing). In October 1984 the Main Stand was destroyed by a fire. The new stand (named City Stand) opened in August 1986 and now has 3,028 seats.

In April 1992 the Barclay Terrace was demolished and by August of that same year the new all-seater Barclay Stand (5,759) was unveiled. Seats, as is common, are in the club colours, but selected yellow seats depict two canaries in the sea of green — a nice variation on the more usual club names. In the

same year Norwich also fitted seats to the existing River End Terrace.

Carrow Road, from which the ground takes its name, winds around the north and west of the ground; the railway line runs from east to west with the BR station nearby, while the River Wensum is to the south.

Notts County

The transformation of Meadow Lane during the 1992 close season astounded many of the ground's critics — three impressive stands seating a total of 13,500 were built in four months at a cost of £3.2 million. The new County Road Stand seats just under 6,000 and, like the one it replaced, sports a simple white gable bearing the club badge and name. At the Meadow Lane End, a 2,000-seater family stand hides the back of a sports complex and club offices, while a new 5,500-seat stand was built on the previously uncovered Spion Kop.

When the Magpies arrived in 1910, Meadow Lane was open ground next to a cattle market. Contractors hastily erected the steelwork and roof of the Main Stand, while a 1,400-seat stand which the club had floated across the river from their previous Trent Bridge home was placed at the south end. This is reported to have survived to become one of the oldest stands in the League before being demolished in 1978.

The remaining two sides of the ground were terracing, the County Road Side having an open stream, Tinkers Brook, running to the Trent which was patrolled by a man armed with a long pole to fish balls out of the water. In 1923, the County Road Stand was built, actually on top of the banking and across Tinkers Brook.

County endured misfortune in the 1940s: they were yet another club to suffer war damage when bombs destroyed the Main Stand in 1941 and

CAPACITY:
18,781

HIGHEST ATTENDANCE:
47,310 v York City,
12 March 1955,
FA Cup 6th Round

CAPACITY 1971:
40,000

damaged the pitch so badly they had to withdraw from wartime football, while in 1946-47 (with prisoners of war used to clear the playing surface of snow) Meadow Lane was flooded as the Trent rose, although not as severely as Forest's City Ground.

Even with promotion to the First Division in 1981, the club realised that gates were unlikely to average more than about 12,000, so they built a sports complex, the Meadow Club, on the site of the wooden stand at the Meadow Lane End, leaving a gap between the goal and the walls. The complex also incorporated changing rooms which had previously been housed in the Main Stand. Seats were installed in the centre of the County Road Stand bringing the mid-1980s capacity to 24,077, including just 3,998 seats.

With its well-thought-out design, Meadow Lane in the 1990s stands as an example to other clubs looking to redevelop existing sites.

Opposite top: Manager Mick Walker surveys a rejuvenated Meadow Lane in 1993.

Opposite: An earlier view of the ground showing the original County Road Stand.

Above: Floodlights illuminate an early-1993 FA Cup tie against Sunderland.

Left: Seen in 1979, the Main Stand was the last side to be redeveloped in the 1990s.

95

Nottingham Forest

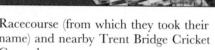

The City Ground's inclusion as a venue for the 1996 European Championships is reward for an ambitious £15 million all-seater redevelopment programme by Nottingham Forest.

The building of two new stands at Trent End and the open Bridgford End (away) are long overdue. The ends of the stadium have long been overshadowed by the Main (west) Stand and Executive (east) Stand on the sides of the City Ground. Forest have always concentrated on upgrading these stands in the past as opposed to developing the areas behind the goals.

Forest eventually settled at the City Ground in 1898 — some 33 nomadic years after their formation. In that time they had seven homes, including Forest Racecourse (from which they took their name) and nearby Trent Bridge Cricket Ground.

The City Ground and Meadow Lane, home of County, are the two closest League grounds in England, with just the River Trent and 400yd separating them. At the time of the

CAPACITY:

22,500 (rising to 30,500 in March 1995)

HIGHEST ATTENDANCE:

49,945 v Manchester United, 28 October 1967, Division One

CAPACITY 1971:

49,000

Top left: The old East Stand, replaced in 1980 by the Executive Stand (Left).

Above: The City Ground in 1925.

Opposite top: The planned redevelopment for 1996 includes stands at the Trent and Bridgford Ends.

Opposite: Extending the open Bridgford End in the late 1950s.

move, indeed up until 1910, the two clubs were even closer, as County were at this time residing at Trent Bridge.

During these early days the clubs frequently 'borrowed' each other's facilities for certain games, especially during their respective spells at the cricket ground, when cricket naturally took preference in the case of fixture clashes.

One further temporary groundshare followed when, in 1947, flooding from the Trent submerged the City Ground in several feet of water. Some years after this damp experience the ground started to take on the form it retained until the recent developments.

A new East Stand was built in 1958 and four years later improvements and re-roofing were carried out on the Main Stand. At this time there were only 6,500 seats in a capacity of 48,000, a further indication of the transformation

the ground had to undergo to become all-seater. On 24 August 1968, during a League match with Leeds United, this stand was entirely gutted by fire. The game was naturally abandoned but all the spectators escaped from the blaze largely uninjured.

Another brief sojourn at Meadow Lane followed during repairs; then, in

1980, on the back of domestic and European success, the new Executive Stand was built in place of the old East Stand. The £2.5 million two-tiered stand, which included a row of executive boxes, increased the seating capacity at the City Ground to just under 15,000.

Oldham Athletic

CAPACITY:

12,500

HIGHEST ATTENDANCE:

47,671 v Sheffield Wednesday,
25 January 1930,
FA Cup 4th Round

CAPACITY 1971:

41,200

Only since their return to football's top
flight in 1991 after a 68-year absence
have Oldham, Greater Manchester's
third-string team behind United and
City, found Boundary Park less than
ample for their needs. They have been
resident there since 1899, previously
playing their home matches at Berry's
Field and then Shiloh (using dressing
rooms as luxurious as a smithy and the
Black Cow Inn), though after a rent
dispute they spent the first few years of
the new century at Hudson Fold.

Promotion to the First Division in
1910 meant increased attendances, and
stands were renovated. In the summer
of 1913, the ground underwent a
complete overhaul with the Rochdale
Road End able to house 18,000. A
stand was built on the south side of the
ground with 1,092 tip-up chairs in the
middle, bringing the capacity to 45,000
at the outbreak of war.

Calamity struck in October 1927 as
work on the Chadderton Road Stand,
nearing completion and scheduled to
accommodate 12,000, had to be
restarted after it was blown down in a
hurricane.

Winning the Ford Sporting League
first prize of £70,000 in 1970-71

*Top right: Oldham's artificial pitch, laid in
1986, was replaced before the team's
promotion in 1991.*

*Above: Boundary Park viewed from the air
in 1968, seven years after the belated
installation of floodlights.*

enabled the replacement of the old
Broadway Stand with the Ford Stand.
Undersoil heating became the next
arrival at Boundary Park, being used in
December 1980 for a game against
Grimsby, and three years later work
commenced in removing the Rochdale
Road End terracing. This is now all-
seating, with 4,600 seats installed at a
cost of £1.9 million.

They may have been the last League
club in Lancashire to install floodlights
(in 1961), but in June 1986 the Latics

became the fourth League ground to
adopt artificial turf when construction
of a new pitch began (at a cost of
£385,000) — one decision made was to
remove the undersoil heating. They
reverted to grass on Football League
orders before regaining top-flight status,
while the 3,600-seater Seton Stand
(costing £1.5 million) helped them
accommodate the crowds which, until
relegation in May 1994, came to watch
them play Premier League football at
Boundary Park.

Oxford United

The Manor Ground became home to Headington United (the forerunner of Oxford) in 1925 when they were still in the Southern League. The first stand went up in 1946 and terracing was laid two years later. Professionalism in 1949 brought rapid development, with £4,000 spent on new stands, terracing and dressing rooms, the capacity increasing to 12,000 by 1950. It was on 18 December of that year when United played their first game under floodlights at the Manor Ground — before any of the current League clubs.

The club have moved home eight times since their formation in 1894, and they are determined to make it nine. The tiny and somewhat cramped Manor Ground is situated in the residential and commercial district of Headington with restricted access and little room for development.

A number of plans for the club's long-term relocation have been put forward, but all have failed following objections from planners and residents. Even the considerable political muscle of former owner and media magnate Robert Maxwell failed in the bid to relocate the club. The most recent proposal is for a 15,000-seater stadium on the edge of the Blackbird Leys housing estate outside the city, which was under consideration in mid-1994.

CAPACITY:

11,000

HIGHEST ATTENDANCE:

22,750 v Preston North End, 29 February 1964, FA Cup 6th Round

CAPACITY 1971:

18,000

Top: The Manor Ground in the 1980s, when Oxford United enjoyed their greatest success.

Above left: Looking over towards the Osler Road side and London Road End in the previous decade.

Plymouth Argyle

CAPACITY:

19,860

HIGHEST ATTENDANCE:

43,596 v Aston Villa,
10 October 1936,
Division Two

CAPACITY 1971:

40,000

Home Park is Britain's most southwesterly League ground. Continue in the same direction and the next football club in your path would be South American.

Its geographical position means it is rarely chosen for showpiece games, although in 1966 seven of England's World Cup-winning team were at Home Park for a Football League XI match against an Irish League XI. In 1977 Manchester United played the 'home' leg of their European Cup Winners' Cup tie against St Etienne in Plymouth, after being banished from Old Trafford by UEFA following crowd trouble in France.

Plymouth moved to Home Park, previously home to Devonport Albion Rugby Club, in 1901. A new stand and concrete terracing in the 1930s followed Plymouth's rise into the Football League. The ground was out of action during World War 2 because of bomb damage and its use by the US military, and Home Park's capacity has since tumbled from 40,000-plus to under 20,000 following increased seating and safety work.

A new 4,000-seater stand for the Devonport End was started in May 1994, with toilets, clubhouse and offices to be built behind. The old covering from the Devonport End will be erected on the away end. An extension on the roof of the Mayflower Stand will allow for 3,000 upper-tier seats, and with extension of the two side bays, seating will be increased by a further 6,000.

Above: Home Park has changed little since this 1967 view, although 1994 development work will see the Peveril End (nearest to the camera) covered at last.

Left: The entrance to the visitors' end and Mayflower Stand.

Portsmouth

CAPACITY:

26,452

HIGHEST ATTENDANCE:

51,385 v Derby County,
26 February 1949,
FA Cup 6th Round

CAPACITY 1971:

46,000

The unkindest cut in many a year occurred at Portsmouth when the Fratton End was cut in half and the top tier of seats removed because of safety regulations. While this has balanced the ground somewhat (the opposite Milton End has always been similarly uncovered), the famous Pompey Chimes often drift away into the sky.

Resident at Fratton Park since 1898, Portsmouth's ground is one of the delights of football. A mock-Tudor cottage is the first sight that greets the visitor in Frogmore Road, set above the gates that lead to the terraces in front. This was one of many stands built by the famed football stadium constructor Archibald Leitch, in 1925. Leitch's trademark, the balcony wall criss-crossed at the front with steel supports, is evident, just as it is at Goodison Park, Roker Park and Ibrox. Also of historical note is that Fratton Park played host to the very first League match to be played under floodlights, in 1956.

Opposite this, the South Stand, is the North Stand; a huge bank of terracing topped with a long and low stand. While the Fratton End is only half of what it used to be, the Milton End remains much the same today as it did when first constructed, but access problems can be experienced when crowds are large.

Fratton Park's 1994 capacity of just over 26,000 is adequate for the First Division, but with moves towards all-seater stadia now under way, Portsmouth's ground has more to lose than most when the terracing is removed. Unless the new stadium at Parkway becomes a reality, the unkind cuts at Fratton Park may have only just begun.

Top: Portsmouth's Frogmore Road entrance is one of British football's more memorable sights.

Left: Fratton Park in 1957, with the Fratton End having just been covered.

FRATTON PARK

Port Vale

'The Wembley of the North' was how Vale Park was intended when work began on the site in 1944. Indeed, an artist's impression of the ground in 1950 showed a stadium that would be capable of holding 70,000 fans and be the envy of every club in the League.

Over 30,000cu yd of earth were removed from the 14-acre site just to level the surface, but in the immediate postwar years building materials were scarce and Vale's grand designs were necessarily modified. The Main Stand was never built; instead a small covered enclosure provides cover for the directors and their guests, sitting either side of a players' entrance which gives an idea of how grand the original plans were. Opposite is the Railway Stand, an impressive-looking structure from a distance; the proposed railway station (echoes of Wembley again) was never built and even the railway line is no longer used.

The Bycars Lane End offered little protection from the elements to those seated in the paddock since the roof barely covered even half of the end. This was finally rectified in the 1990s with a roof bought from Chester City when they vacated Sealand Road. For many years, however, even half a cover was better than no cover at all, which the occupants of the Hamil Road End still had to endure.

Port Vale never got their capacity up to 70,000, the closest they came being the 50,000 packed in for a Cup tie with Aston Villa in 1960. Today that capacity is down to 22,359, of which just over 12,000 is seating. But Port Vale still have the scope for further development if success on the pitch can be maintained. Until then, 'The Wembley of the North' must necessarily remain a dream.

CAPACITY:

22,359

HIGHEST ATTENDANCE:

50,000 v Aston Villa,
20 February 1960,
FA Cup 5th Round

CAPACITY 1971:

50,000

Top: Vale Park in 1991, looking across to the Railway Stand.

Above: This view from the top of the Hamil Road banking shows the players' tunnel at right, overlooked by the directors' enclosure.

Preston North End

As the first ever Football League Champions in 1888-89 (they also won the FA Cup that year) Preston's place in football history is secure. Yet a proud past has not made the club afraid to look forward; they were one of a handful of clubs to experiment with synthetic grass during the 1980s — and, in 1994, were the last club to have it removed.

The current West Stand was built in 1906, the North End was extended and covered in 1921, the Pavilion and a new stand at the Town End went up in 1934 and two years later the South Pavilion was erected. During World War 2 prisoners of war were held at Deepdale.

A total of £500,000 was spent on safety work in the late 1970s, but there have been no major changes during the last few years although a new Ground Control Room has been built and there have been improvements to gates and fences. The West Stand is similar in construction to the ill-fated Bradford Main Stand and will need redevelopment. This neared reality when Preston Council, the club's landlords, offered them a new long-term lease in early 1994 and plans were announced to rebuild the ground in a £10 million scheme modelled on the Luigi Ferraris home of Italian giants Sampdoria and Genoa.

CAPACITY:

16,249

HIGHEST ATTENDANCE:

42,684 v Arsenal,
23 April 1938,
Division One

CAPACITY 1971:

40,100

Of England's League clubs, only Stoke City have been at their current ground longer than Preston. Football was played at Deepdale in 1881 while the Victoria Ground was in use in 1878. Some historians may feel inclined to give the honour to Preston, since the cricket and athletics club which gave birth to the football club was at Deepdale from 1875.

Top: Deepdale in 1991 combined a futuristic synthetic pitch with an old-fashioned structure, the West Stand, similar to the ill-fated Bradford City Main Stand. Also visible is the Spion Kop (right).

Left: Nearly 20 years earlier, a packed South Pavilion watches North End take on Birmingham City.

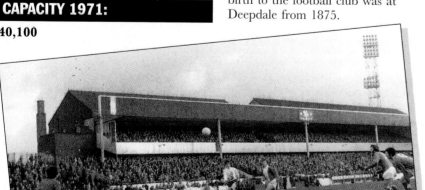

DEEPDALE

Queens Park Rangers

In total QPR have moved home more often than any other League club — a staggering 14 times since their formation in 1885, although sometimes returning to previous grounds. The club first moved to Loftus Road in 1917, although tenure has not been continuous as they have had two short spells at the now-demolished White City, the latest coming in 1962 (the club's record attendance was recorded here: 41,097 v Leeds United, 9 January 1932). Add to this list the temporary use of White City in 1908, Stamford Bridge (1915), and Highbury (for one game in 1930) and QPR could rightly be dubbed the most restless of League clubs.

The only stand at Loftus Road (officially named the Rangers Stadium) in 1917 was a structure QPR transported from a previous ground at Park Royal. A cover was erected over the Loftus Road End in 1938, and

concrete terraces laid ten years later when the club purchased the freehold of the ground.

The two-tier South Africa Road Stand went up on the Popular Side in 1968 and four years later the Main Stand was replaced by a single-tier 5,000-seater structure. In 1980 a new stand went up on the Loftus Road End

and within a year executive boxes had been installed and the School End developed with a similarly styled stand.

In 1981 QPR became the first British League club to lay synthetic grass, but their progressive outlook brought only criticism. Other clubs such as Luton, Oldham and Preston enjoyed relatively more success with the

CAPACITY:

19,300

HIGHEST ATTENDANCE:

**35,353 v Leeds Utd,
27 April 1974,
Division One**

CAPACITY 1971:

35,000

artificial turf because of the lessons learned by QPR, who reverted to 'real' grass in 1988.

In 1992 QPR spent £1.5 million on safety measures, including major escape staircases and electrical works. A year later the terracing at the School End was converted to seats (1,392) at a cost of £600,000. Seating was increased by a further 2,900 the next year when £1.6 million was spent on installing seats in the Loftus Road terrace and the east and west paddocks.

Opposite top: Loftus Road in 1992, the year Rangers spent £1.5 million on ground improvements.

Opposite: An aerial view in 1928.

Left: A packed School End observes a 1973 west London derby between QPR and Fulham.

Below: Looking across to the Loftus Road End terracing in 1978, which two years later was converted into a double-decker stand.

Reading

CAPACITY:

12,200

HIGHEST ATTENDANCE:

33,042 v Brentford,
19 February 1927,
FA Cup 5th Round

CAPACITY 1971:

27,200

Elm Park faced the most ignominious of ends in 1983 when the then Oxford chairman Robert Maxwell proposed a merger with Reading to form the Thames Valley Royals, with the new ground somewhere between the two towns. Supporters' opposition and a new chairman at Elm Park ended the merger plans — and, although the club have expressed an interest in finding a new ground in the 1990s, it will at least be for the Royals of Reading.

Reading have played at Elm Park since 1896, one of their earlier grounds being at Reading Cricket Club. The Main Stand was built in 1925, five years after Reading joined the Football League as founder members of Division Three. The Tilehurst Road (South Bank) terraces opposite were covered and extended after World War 2.

A sum of £160,000 was spent on safety work during the mid-1980s, but the most recent development at Elm Park has been the provision of 18 executive boxes at the rear of the North Stand. Further development depends on the success or otherwise of their aspiration to move and their continued progress in the League.

Top: Elm Park in 1954 remained substantially similar four decades later.

Left: The view from the Tilehurst End terraces, looking towards the similarly uncovered Reading End.

Rotherham United

The original occupants of Millmoor were Rotherham County, who arrived at the site in 1907 from the Red House Ground where the pitch was so uneven the club were barred from entering the FA Cup! County joined the Second Division in 1919 and six years later joined forces with Rotherham Town to become Rotherham United.

The new club's ground is deep in the heart of the industrial north; indeed it would be difficult for Millmoor to get any closer, hemmed in as it is by scrap yards on three sides of the ground.

The Main Stand was the first to be built not long after the amalgamation of County and Town, followed by a small cover placed over the terracing on the opposite side along Millmoor Lane, the thoroughfare from which the ground derives its name.

The Railway End was the first to be covered, in 1957, followed 11 years later by the Tivoli End. The only other development at the ground of any particular note was the construction of an extended roof over the Main Stand in the mid-1960s and the conversion of the Millmoor Lane side to seating and a new roof in 1982.

The Millmoor Lane side is actually three separate entities; the centre section which is covered and all-seater, an open terrace to the left and to the right, and another seating section covered by a roof on stilts. The Main Stand, meanwhile, is yet another stand that fails to run the entire length of the pitch.

The curious nature of the ground is probably in keeping with its location, for it is possible to see the contents of the yards that surround Millmoor. Only the pitch offers sight of anything alive and growing!

CAPACITY:

13,037

HIGHEST ATTENDANCE:

25,000 v Sheffield Utd, 15 December 1952, Division Two and 25,000 v Sheffield Wednesday, 26 January 1952, Division Two

CAPACITY 1971:

24,000

Millmoor has changed little in the years between these two pictures of the Tivoli End in 1969 (Above) and 1992 (Top). The roof of the Main Stand may be discerned to the left of the later picture.

107

Scunthorpe United

CAPACITY:

9,183

HIGHEST ATTENDANCE:

**23,935 v Portsmouth,
30 January 1954,
FA Cup 4th Round
(Old Showground).
8,775 v Rotherham United,
1 May 1989,
Division Four (Glanford Park)**

CAPACITY 1971:

27,000 (Old Showground)

In 1988 Scunthorpe United became the first League club in modern times to move to a new purpose-built ground when they took up residence at the £2.5 million Glanford Park.

The new ground was opened by HRH Princess Alexandra on 14 August, for a match between Scunthorpe and a Football League XI managed by Graham Taylor, who grew up in the town. Kevin Keegan and Ray Clemence, who both started their careers at Scunthorpe, were also there to add their support. The match referee was Graham Alson, vice-chairman of the club.

Glanford Park is situated one and a half miles outside the town centre on a greenfield site. On the north is the

Opposite top: The Glanford Stand, pictured in the summer of 1988.

Opposite below: The Old Showground from the air five years earlier and (Bottom) in the 1950s, showing the stand that burnt down in 1958.

Left: Scunthorpe's new ground was funded by the Old Showground's sale to a supermarket chain. The last regular-season League game at the old ground (programme Below) took place on 2 May 1988.

Bottom: Glanford Park takes shape, with the old ground's floodlights on the horizon.

Rodmill Terrace, with terracing for 2,773; the Glanford Stand (west), which also has restaurant facilities, has seating for 2,250 and the Clugston Stand (east) seats 2,400. In 1990 1,678 seats replaced the terracing on the Yorkshire Electricity Stand, reducing the capacity at the new ground from 11,266 to its current 9,183. There are also nine executive boxes.

Glanford Park opened just over two years after the club, following the Bradford fire, first announced their desire to move from the Old Showground. The sale of the site to a supermarket chain was enough to pay off the club's debts and finance the new stadium, which took 11 months to build.

The Old Showground was home to Scunthorpe for nearly 90 years. United first played there in 1899 and the ground was chosen as home when United amalgamated with North Lindsey United in 1910 to form Scunthorpe & Lindsey United.

Grimsby Town, who were a First Division club at the outbreak of World War 2, used the ground for some of their wartime matches. In 1942 the Old Showground was used for the FA Cup Northern Section semi-final second leg between Grimsby and Sunderland.

The new East Stand, which went up following a fire on the east side of the Old Showground in 1958, was significant in that it was the first cantilever stand ever to be built in Britain — pre-dating the next cantilever (at Hillsborough) by three years.

The last game was played at the Old Showground in May 1988 and it brought added tears when Scunthorpe lost in the Fourth Division promotion play-offs.

Sheffield United

CAPACITY:

32,000

HIGHEST ATTENDANCE:

68,287 v Leeds Utd,
15 February 1936,
FA Cup 5th Round

CAPACITY 1971:

55,000

side of the ground, directly opposite the cricket pavilion. Over the next 30 years the football club built up the two ends available to it and during the 1930s Bramall Lane could hold 68,000 people.

Like Old Trafford, Bramall Lane suffered greatly during World War 2, with 10 bombs causing damage that took eight years to rectify. Once the football side of the ground was brought up to scratch, the death-knell began to sound for cricket and Yorkshire CCC played their last match at Bramall Lane in August 1973. Two years later, a brand new cantilevered stand seating nearly 8,000 was in place and opened for the first time on 16 August 1975. This stand now contains the offices and dressing rooms, those in the John Street Stand having remained unused ever since. Other sections of that stand are also unused, closed by various legislation over the years.

The Bramall Lane Stand is a rather soulless tall stand with seating for 3,000 on the top tier and standing room for 7,000 underneath, although the latter figure is obviously drastically reduced by the all-seating legislation. The top tier, however, provides an excellent view of the pitch.

At the opposite end, the Kop is now all-seater and has a brand new roof to keep its patrons dry. White seats amongst the predominantly red seats spell out the letters 'SUFC'. That effectively leaves only the John Street Stand in need of attention, but one suspects it will be a case of making do with the existing structure until sufficient funds are in place to build a new stand similar to the cantilevered South Stand.

Opposite top: Bramall Lane in 1978, looking across the ground to the cricket pavilion.

Opposite bottom: This 1966 aerial view clearly shows the proximity of the football and cricket grounds.

Top: The 8,000-seat South Stand was opened in 1975, and is seen here from the street and (Above) the pitch. The Kop (left) is now seated.

Though Bramall Lane is no longer home to both a League football club and a first-class cricket venue, there is another honour which the ground will retain for ever; on 14 October 1878, It hosted the very first game to be played under floodlights. A crowd of 20,000 (although only 12,000 paid admission) watched two local teams play under four lights powered by two generators. The light was said to be the equivalent of 30,000 candles.

Organised sport first came to Bramall Lane in 1854 with the formation of a Sheffield Cricket Club which secured a 99-year lease from the Duke of Norfolk. Yorkshire CCC made their first appearance at the ground in 1855 and football came along seven

years later when Sheffield FC played Hallam in December 1862. In 1883 England played Scotland at the ground, while Bramall Lane hosted an FA Cup semi-final in 1889.

At this point the cricket club formed Sheffield United, and within a decade had taken their first (and so far only) League Championship in 1898. Such success prompted the formation of a limited liability company, the Sheffield United Cricket and Football Club, which in turn purchased Bramall Lane from the Duke of Norfolk for £10,134.

While the football club had used the cricket facilities for the first ten years of its existence, separate offices and dressing rooms were constructed at the turn of the century on the John Street

Sheffield Wednesday

Hillsborough has become the name synonymous with the tragedy which occurred on 17 April 1989. If it was the Bradford fire in 1985 which brought change to our sporting stadia, then it was the events at Hillsborough, on the afternoon when 95 football supporters lost their lives, that forced a transformation.

The Taylor Report, produced to ensure there was no repeat of that tragedy, was published in January 1990. Old stadia, old-style thinking and old complacency were at an end. Despite many pleas of poverty, clubs were given until August 1994 to bring their grounds fully into line with Taylor's recommendations.

For some this meant almost complete redevelopment of the ground; others sought out brand new stadia, while many simply shut down unsafe sections of their ground until money was available for redevelopment. The Taylor deadline dictated that many redevelopment programmes could not be completed during the close season — traditionally the period set aside for major work on grounds. During the

CAPACITY:

36,020

HIGHEST ATTENDANCE:

72,841 v Manchester City, 17 February 1934, FA Cup 5th Round

CAPACITY 1971:

60,000

early 1990s it became commonplace, especially in the top two divisions (where tighter time constraints were imposed by Taylor), for matches to be played with only three, sometimes even two sides of the ground open.

Regardless of the option taken towards compliance, the face of football grounds was changing dramatically all over the country. Nowhere was this more true than at Hillsborough, which simply had to become a flag bearer for the new safety standards.

The previous huge capacity (in 1971, Hillsborough had been able to accommodate 60,000) became a memory as Wednesday strove to meet the all-seater requirements of the Taylor Report. In 1991, 2,610 seats were put into the lower section of the West Stand, (the Leppings Lane End) and a new roof added. Over £1.5 million was spent giving the ageing South Stand a new roof and seating in 1992 (2,733 seats in the lower section and 4,638 seats in the upper section). Seating (11,211) was installed in the Spion Kop in the summer of 1993 at a

cost of £860,000; an end where the terracing had been extended upwards in 1986 to accommodate a £1 million roof and create 5,000 extra standing places. The changes gave Wednesday a capacity of 36,020.

Despite that fateful day in 1989, football's authorities have continued to recognise Hillsborough as a major match venue, and there was

Opposite: Hillsborough from the air in 1980.

Top: This 1993 view looks over the Kop, which received a new roof seven years earlier.

Inset top: Liverpool manager Kenny Dalglish watches the 1989 tragedy unfold.

Above: The FA Cup semi-final between Coventry and Leeds two years earlier passed off, like so many before it, without incident.

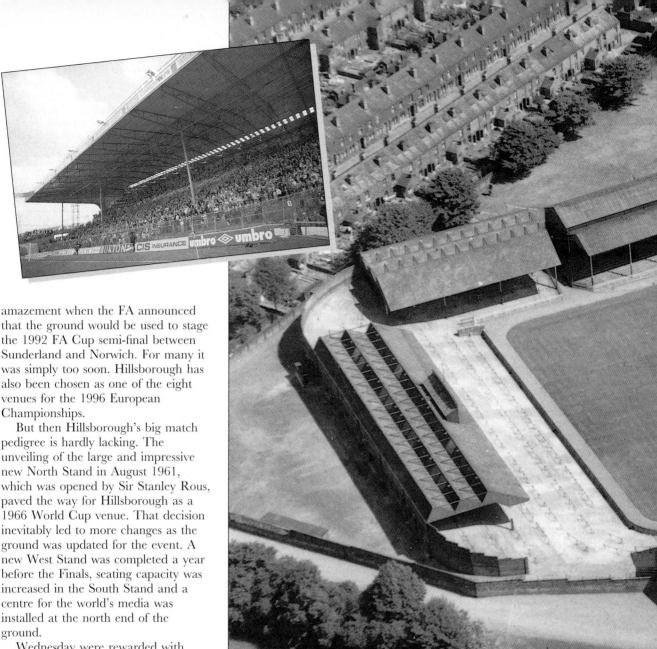

amazement when the FA announced that the ground would be used to stage the 1992 FA Cup semi-final between Sunderland and Norwich. For many it was simply too soon. Hillsborough has also been chosen as one of the eight venues for the 1996 European Championships.

But then Hillsborough's big match pedigree is hardly lacking. The unveiling of the large and impressive new North Stand in August 1961, which was opened by Sir Stanley Rous, paved the way for Hillsborough as a 1966 World Cup venue. That decision inevitably led to more changes as the ground was updated for the event. A new West Stand was completed a year before the Finals, seating capacity was increased in the South Stand and a centre for the world's media was installed at the north end of the ground.

Wednesday were rewarded with three matches from a group that included West Germany, Spain, Switzerland and Argentina plus the West Germany v Uruguay (4-0) quarter-final.

Hillsborough had come of age despite being so near to Bramall Lane which, when Wednesday had first moved, was hosting not only international football matches but Test cricket as well. Indeed, before their move to Hillsborough Wednesday had been obliged to use their neighbours' facilities for certain 'big games', and there was even talk of a groundsharing arrangement until Wednesday plumped for their own nearby site.

Owlerton, as Hillsborough was known until 1912, opened for sporting business on 2 September 1899 for a Second Division game with Chesterfield.

A new South Stand was completed in January 1914, replacing a stand which had been transported from Wednesday's previous home at Olive Grove when they had moved. Partial cover was gradually put up for supporters on the west and north bank terracing but the east (Kop) remained open banking and most of the record 72,841 who watched Manchester City's visit for an FA Cup 5th Round tie in 1934 would have faced the February elements without protection.

Opposite top: A nearly full Spion Kop as viewed from the Hillsborough pitch.

Above: This fascinating aerial view from 1951 shows Hillsborough without floodlights and with only one covered (Leppings Lane) end.

Left: League action in 1966, the year Hillsborough was chosen as a venue for the World Cup. The South Stand seen here dated from 1914.

Shrewsbury Town

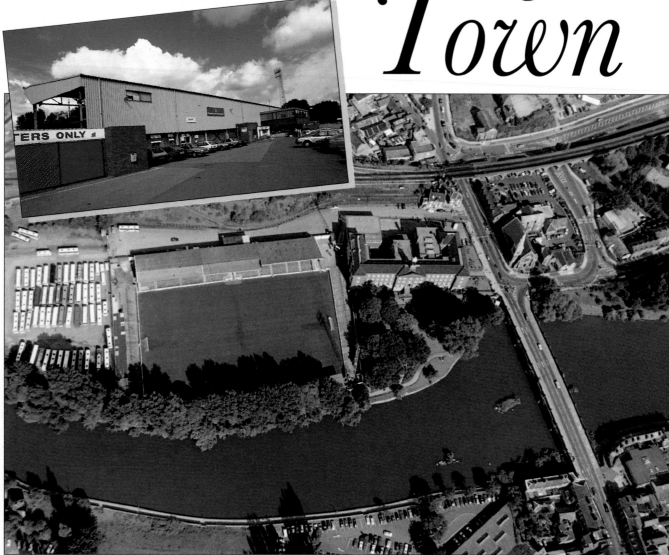

CAPACITY:

7,500

HIGHEST ATTENDANCE:

**18,917 v Walsall,
26 April 1961,
Division Three**

CAPACITY 1971:

20,050

Every football ground in the country has a particular story to tell and Shrewsbury's aptly named Gay Meadow is no exception. Until 1986, a man was employed by the club to retrieve stray footballs from the River Severn and return them to the club for the princely sum of 25p a time. This was something of a hazardous job, for 500yd down the river from the stadium is a weir.

Shrewsbury came to Gay Meadow in 1910 and built a small wooden grandstand on the east side with small huts as dressing rooms. New dressing rooms were built in 1921 and a new Centre Stand was constructed around these in 1922 when the Mayor performed the opening ceremony.

The 1930s saw considerable activity at the ground with the Station End and Riverside being covered, the terracing being concreted over and a new wing added to the Centre Stand. After World

War 2, therefore, Gay Meadow was a homely ground and well able to deal with the crowds that would attend Midland League matches. In 1948 the ground was chosen as the venue for the amateur international between England and Wales and two years later, following the extension of the Football League by four clubs, Shrewsbury were elected to Division Three North.

League status may have brought extra interest but it did not necessarily mean extra revenue; it was possible to watch the match from the opposite bank of the river until the Riverside cover was completed and tall trees planted. Today the Riverside is a narrow stretch of terracing with a low cover, dwarfed by the trees immediately behind. Visitors are accommodated in the Station End, another narrow stretch of terracing. At least the visitors have some cover, for the opposite end is open owing to the Wakeman School immediately behind.

Visitors to Gay Meadow hoping for a glimpse of the famous coracle will be sadly out of luck: either the trees have got too big or defenders are much more careful with their clearances.

Opposite top: The Wakeman Stand, one of two wings of the Centre Stand.

Opposite: The ground from the air in 1992 and (Below) sixty years earlier. Most of the development the stadium has seen took place in the 1930s.

Southampton

Southampton were dealt a particularly hard blow by the Taylor Report. For years, objections from planners and the public and red tape had delayed the club's plans to relocate. Taylor's deadline simply came too soon for Southampton. They must spend money on all-seater conversion if they are to stay at the Dell, but their continued desire for a move means that this could simply be money down the short-term drain.

A planning application to move to a 25,000-seater stadium at Stoneham, a 65-acre site which is planned to include a leisure complex, athletics track and parking for 5,500 cars was rejected in October 1993. A decision on the club's appeal against the verdict is due during the 1994-95 season.

While plans for a long-term solution to Southampton's future continued, however, the club had to make sure the Dell was up to standard. A new 1,300-seater stand has been built at the Archer's Road End and more seating added to the East and West Stand paddock terraces. The summer of 1994 also brought a new stand to replace the previously open and somewhat awkwardly-shaped Milton Road terrace.

CAPACITY:

15,000

HIGHEST ATTENDANCE:

31,044 v Manchester United,
8 October 1969,
Division One

CAPACITY 1971:

31,000

The redevelopment of the West Stand, planned for 1996, is dependent on the outcome of the club's search for a new home.

After 12 years at the Antelope Ground and a season at the County Cricket Ground, Southampton moved the short distance to the Dell in 1898. A stand on either side and open terracing behind the goals gave a capacity of 20,000 for the ground's first match, a Southern League fixture against Brighton. In 1901, while still a Southern League venue, the Dell became an international venue when it was chosen to host the England v Ireland fixture (England won 3-0).

The club's decision to join the newly formed Football League Division Three in 1920 prompted a number of changes at the Dell. The two-tiered West Stand went up in 1926 and a new East Stand was built three years later, following a

fire in the stand on the opposite side of the ground.

The club briefly used Fratton Park, home of coastal rivals Portsmouth, during World War 2, when a bomb burst a water drain, causing flooding. Such groundsharing is unlikely in the 1990s, but the Dell's cluttered city-centre site is simply unsuitable for a top-level professional football club.

Opposite: This unusual view of the Dell from 1990 looks from the East Stand to the West Stand.

Opposite inset: The Archers Road and (Below) Milton Road Ends in 1966. Both have now been replaced by stands.

Bottom: Even in 1935, the Dell was uncomfortably cramped by its city-centre surroundings.

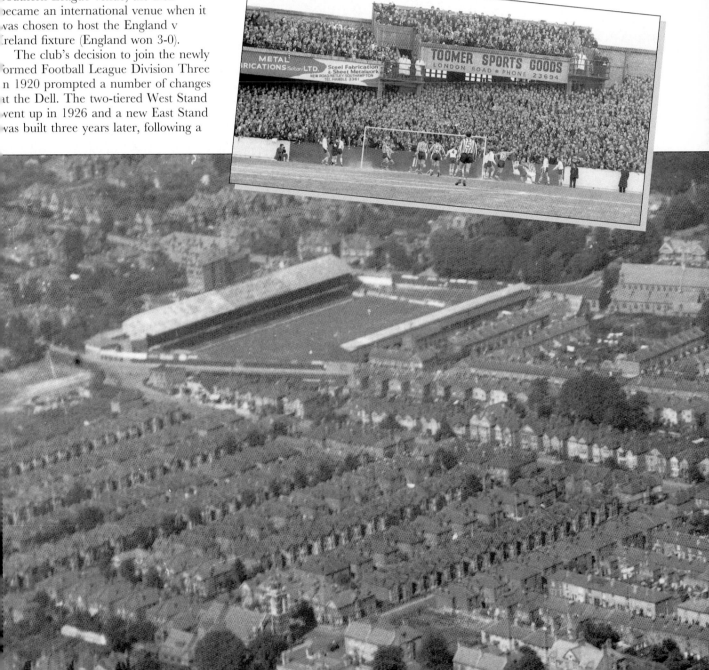

Southend United

CAPACITY:

12,000

HIGHEST ATTENDANCE:

**31,036 v Liverpool,
10 January 1979,
FA Cup 3rd Round**

CAPACITY 1971:

39,466

When Southend United were looking for a site of their own in the 1950s, they were drawn to Roots Hall, by coincidence their first home. There were considerable differences between the Roots Hall of 1906 and that of today, not least of which was the fact that the pitch was then a good 50ft higher. Southend United remained until 1919 when they moved to the Kursaal Ground, next door to the famous fairground site, and a year later League football arrived in the town for the first time.

Top: Roots Hall as viewed from the South Bank, looking at the North Bank and East Stand. Note the latter's enthusiastic market advertisement.

Above right: The Kursaal Ground, Southend's home from 1919 to 1934.

Opposite top: The West Stand in 1993.

Opposite: An aerial view of Roots Hall from 1935, the year after their return.

The Kursaal Ground was home for the next 15 years, with a ground record attendance of 17,000 before moving into the Southend Greyhound Stadium in 1934. Two years later United attracted that venue's record crowd, 22,862 watching the clash with Spurs.

Although Southend did not vacate the Greyhound Stadium until 1955, work had been going on at Roots Hall to prepare it for their return since 1953. The land had been bought by the supporters and they were also responsible for much of the

development at the site over the next few years. That they made a good job is apparent, for Sir Stanley Rous, then Secretary of the FA, was in attendance at the first match, a Third Division South game against Norwich.

The ground itself was of fairly basic design — an open end of terracing, a Main Stand that was relatively small even by 1950s standards and which was subsequently extended in 1967, a slightly bigger stand on the opposite side and a covered terrace at the other end. Since Southend are one of the last

League clubs to have moved into their current stadium, little additional work is evident. Indeed, the only changes a visitor from 40 years ago would notice is how much of the ground has had to be closed down as a result of safety regulations, though by August 1994 the ground was all-seater with a two-tier stand on the South Bank, the West Stand being extended north and south and hospitality boxes being incorporated into the Main Stand. Outside the ground the giant car park is used twice a week for an open-air market, bringing in vital revenue for the football club.

Despite the relatively short time Southend United have been at Roots Hall the club would like to move and construct a custom-built stadium elsewhere but have thus far found local opposition an insurmountable barrier. In one sense this sums up the story of Southend as a town over the past 50 years or so — the Kursaal has gone, the Pier has gone and now the football club would like to go. In the meantime, they make do with as much of Roots Hall as safety regulations allow.

Stoke City

VICTORIA GROUND

Stoke City have been at their ground longer than any other club in Britain. England's second oldest club first played at the Victoria Ground in 1878, when it was known as the Athletic Club Ground.

The club have just two major trophies (the League Cup in 1971-72 and Second Division Championship in 1992-93) to show for their long tenure at the Victoria Ground, but while it remains their home Stoke are assured of a continuing place in the history of football grounds.

Despite being original members of the Football League in 1888, Stoke have not enjoyed an unbroken run in the competition, twice having failed to get re-elected. When the club was re-admitted to Division Two status in 1919 the Victoria Ground boasted a Main Stand (which was rebuilt during the next decade), and a smaller wooden stand opposite. In 1930 the Boothen End was terraced and covered, and five years later the 5,000-seater Butler Street Stand erected. This stand was used by the army during World War 2.

A new Main Stand and dressing rooms were completed in time for the start of the 1963-64 season. In the early 1970s, a new roof was added to the Butler Street Stand to replace the original cover which had been destroyed by a gale. Stoke played one game at Port Vale's ground following the destruction of the roof. The two-tiered Stoke End Stand was opened in 1979, providing 4,000 seats plus standing in a paddock section. The two floodlights at this end of the ground had to be replaced at the same time.

Twice in the 1980s the club was unsuccessful in obtaining planning permission for a supermarket on the site of the Victoria Ground. A groundshare scheme with Port Vale at a new stadium was the reported outcome had the deal gone through.

The biggest change to the Victoria Ground in recent years has been the installation of 25 executive boxes in the Butler Street Stand, but with the current seating capacity of below 10,000 major changes are on the way. Under the conditions of the Taylor Report Stoke have until August 1996 to make the Victoria Ground all-seater.

Opposite top: A winger's-eye view of the Victoria Ground, looking across to the Stoke End and Butler Street Stand.

Opposite below: The Main Stand, development of which was completed in 1963.

Below: The stadium in the 1990s, as seen from the Boothen End.

Below inset: The Stoke End was still uncovered when Chelsea visited the Victoria Ground in early 1974.

Sunderland

Despite having spent £2 million on improving Roker Park in 1992, Sunderland announced plans the same year for a new £75 million out-of-town development, the future of which was still in the balance two years later. Prior to opening Roker Park in September 1898, they had ironically spent the longest spell of their early nomadic existence at a ground called Newcastle Road! Had they been able to purchase the freehold of the property in 1897 they might still be there, but fortunately for Sunderland followers they were able to find an alternative location the same year.

Roker Park's 30,000 spectators were initially housed in a single-deck grandstand, a Clock Stand opposite and two open ends of terracing. Roker Park gained its early notoriety for the prevalence of bad behaviour from spectators; the ground was closed for one match in 1903 following the stoning of the visiting Wednesday team and there were pitch invasions in 1909 (when a police horse was stabbed) and 1912 when over 13,000 above and beyond the ground's capacity were packed inside.

Having purchased the site outright in 1908, Sunderland began expanding the ground, beginning with the Roker End and a strange, propped-up terracing bank in 1913 which brought the capacity up to 50,000; the opposite end was re-terraced in 1925.

CAPACITY:

28,500

HIGHEST ATTENDANCE:

75,118 v Derby County,
8 March 1933,
FA Cup 6th Round replay

CAPACITY 1971:

58,000

The two side stands are the work of one man — Archibald Leitch. He built his first, the Main Stand in 1929 and it features the Leitch trademark of a criss-crossed balcony wall with one vital difference — every ground he had worked on was for a club that had blue as the predominant colour in their kit; Sunderland's was red, and so the balcony is painted red. Seven years later, Leitch built the new Clock Stand which ran the entire length of the pitch and could hold 15,500 in two sections of terracing.

After World War 2 the upper section of the Main Stand was converted to seating, the only major alteration to the ground until the World Cup arrived in 1966. A roof was raised over the Fulwell End and temporary seats fitted, as they were in both paddocks. The upper section of the Clock Stand was also seated and the pitch extended by three yards, but the most impressive structure was the new club offices constructed behind the Main Stand.

The propped terracing at the Roker End survived until 1982 when safety requirements necessitated its removal and a reduction in the standing capacity from 17,000 to under half that figure. Even though the end is now 'squared off', finances were not available to provide cover.

Although the temporary seats have been removed from the Fulwell End, there is very little change to Roker Park as it would have appeared to the players in Group Four of the World Cup in 1966. Nor is there likely to be if the new 48,000-capacity stadium becomes a reality. Should Sunderland return to the Premier Division meanwhile, then one would expect to see the former temporary seats in the Fulwell End returned on a more permanent basis, which would then leave the Roker End — evenly split between home and visiting supporters — to be seated and/or covered.

Opposite top: Roker Park in 1936, showing the propped Roker End terracing (nearest camera) which was not modified until 1982 and the newly-built Clock Stand (to the left).

Opposite: Looking across the pitch towards the Fulwell End in 1992.

Top: The Clock Stand and Fulwell End in 1979, and the Main Stand (Above) in 1992.

Swansea City

As one of only a handful of senior clubs in Wales, Swansea has hosted numerous big matches and internationals, including European and World Cup games. The Vetch Field, however, has suffered in this respect because of Ninian Park's location in the capital and Wrexham's role as the birthplace of the Welsh FA. The renewed use of Cardiff's National Stadium for football in recent years has further restricted Swansea's role in staging showpiece matches.

Football was played at the Vetch Field as early as the 1890s but the professional Swansea Town (the club became Swansea City in 1970) first played there in 1912. A Main Stand was built on the south side a year later and in 1925 the North Bank terracing was built. This was covered in 1959. The double-decker West Stand was built in 1927.

The £800,000 East Stand, incorporating offices, was opened in 1981 to celebrate the club's astonishing rise from Fourth to First Division in just four seasons.

The Football Trust gave a grant of £500,000 to Swansea in 1993 to help with the cost of a new cover and seating for the North Bank, by which time the club was struggling at the lower end of the Second Division and attracting crowds of around 3,500-4,000.

CAPACITY:

16,540

HIGHEST ATTENDANCE:

**32,796 v Arsenal,
17 February 1968,
FA Cup 4th Round**

CAPACITY 1971:

35,000

Above: Swansea's Vetch Field ground as it was in 1921, when the Main Stand offered the only covered accommodation.

Right: Looking towards the futuristic East Stand, completed in 1981. The by-now antiquated Main Stand is to the right.

Swindon Town

CAPACITY:

19,000

HIGHEST ATTENDANCE:

32,000 v Arsenal,
15 January 1972,
FA Cup 3rd Round

CAPACITY 1971:

27,500

Swindon took up residency of the County Ground in 1895, but reached football's top flight (briefly) only in 1993. Playing on what is now a cricket pitch, their early years were successful enough for them to be able to build a stadium alongside. By 1911, terraces had been laid out and a full-length grandstand built.

The Shrivenham Road Side was covered in 1932 and six years later the Town End covered terrace (then the Hotel End) was opened with the supporters' club footing the £4,300 bill. During World War 2, the ground was transformed into a prisoner of war camp, with huts situated on the pitch.

The Shrivenham Road Side welcomed a stand in 1958, bought from the Aldershot military tattoo, while the original Main Stand was replaced by the North Stand in 1971.

The 1975 Safety of Sports Grounds Act forced Swindon to close the upper tier of the Shrivenham Road Stand because exits led only from the rear seats. Terracing was ordered to be resurfaced and the North Stand had to be fitted with new exits from the front rows on to the pitch. The Town End

Stand, designated a family stand, had seats installed.

A total of 1,750 seats added to the North Stand upped the County Ground's capacity to over 18,000, while the summer of 1994 was scheduled to see the Shrivenham Road and Stratton Bank Stands rebuilt, marginally increasing the maximum possible attendance at the homely Wiltshire ground.

Top left: The County Ground's North Stand replaced the old Main Stand in 1971.

Above: An aerial view taken that same year. The Shrivenham Road Stand which faced it was rebuilt in 1994.

Tottenham Hotspur

Tottenham had already been at White Hart Lane (originally known as High Road Ground) for ten years when they were elected to the Football League Division Two in 1908. They had enjoyed success during their early years in the Southern League, winning that competition in their first season at White Hart Lane and becoming the last non-League club to win the FA Cup when they beat Sheffield United 3-1 in a replay in 1901. But it was entry to the national league that prompted the first major development at the ground.

The new West Stand, replacing a simple wooden structure, was opened at the start of the 1909-10 season, the club's first in Division One, and held 9,000 spectators (5,000 seated). Tottenham's famous symbol, the ball and cockerel, emerged at this time when it was added to the new stand. The size of the banking at each end was also extended and the terracing on the east side was later increased.

Following World War 1, during which time the ground was used as a rifle range, Spurs built two covered terrace stands at the Park Lane End and the Paxton Road End. In 1936 the club began work on an ambitious new

CAPACITY:
34,000

HIGHEST ATTENDANCE:
**75,038 v Sunderland,
5 March 1938,
FA Cup 6th Round**

CAPACITY 1971:
56,000

5,000-capacity East Stand, which meant a row of houses had to be demolished. With this was born the Shelf, home to Spurs' most vociferous fans. On the back of on-field success seating was added to the rear of the South and North Stands in the 1960s, but that remained the only major change to the ground until 1980, when work began on a new West Stand.

Costing over £4 million the West Stand provided offices, players' facilities and 72 executive boxes in addition to seating for over 6,000. Sir Stanley Rous officially opened the new stand on 6 February 1982 and the team responded in style with a 6-1 win over visitors Wolves.

At the start of the 1990s Spurs carried out refurbishment of the East Stand and at the end of 1992 the North Stand was re-roofed and the paddock seated. Work on seating the South Stand paddock began in April 1994.

Opposite top: White Hart Lane in 1923, a far cry from the all-seated stadium of the 1990s (Opposite below).

Top: The expensive West Stand, opened in 1982, incorporated 72 executive boxes and replaced the 1909 version (seen Bottom left in 1967).

Above: The East Stand, contsructed between the wars to hold 15,000.

Tranmere Rovers

CAPACITY:

17,500 (on completion of new stand at Bebington Kop)

HIGHEST ATTENDANCE:

**24,424 v Stoke City,
5 February 1972,
FA Cup 4th Round**

CAPACITY 1971:

35,000

The shadow of Tranmere's more illustrious neighbours Everton and Liverpool has undoubtedly stunted the growth of the club's team and ground in the past. However, following a takeover from Wirral businessman Peter Johnson in 1987 Rovers declared their

ambitions to rise above their position as Merseyside's 'third' club both on and off the pitch. Originally the plans were for a £12 million, 20,000-seater stadium to be developed gradually up to the turn of the century but the Taylor Report accelerated the timescale.

The last few years have seen many changes at Prenton Park — new floodlights, refurbishment and fire-proofing of the Main Stand, new terraces, entrances and turnstiles, five new executive suites and electronic scoreboard — but nothing compares to developments in 1994.

There are 3,600 seats in the Main Stand and a further 2,400 will be added in the paddock area. New stands at Borough Road and the Cow Shed

End will each provide 2,500 seats and a 7,000-seater stand will be built at Bebington Kop during the 1994-95 season. Completion of the all-seater stadium is scheduled for early 1995.

Tranmere moved to Prenton Park in 1912, although they had played at a nearby ground known by the same name since 1896 and three other grounds prior to that. The nearby docks meant the ground experienced numerous bombing attacks during World War 2 and was used by the military for anti-aircraft operations.

The roof on the Borough Road Stand, one of the bombing casualties, was replaced after the war, the Cow Shed was built in 1956, and floodlights

Opposite left: Prenton Park pictured in 1967, with the old Grandstand, demolished the following year, in the background.

Opposite right: Its replacement cost only £80,000 to build and was much acclaimed.

Above: Tranmere's ground from the air in 1991 as redevelopment began.

Inset left: Seen in 1978, the gabled Cow Shed End has now been replaced by a seated stand.

erected two years later. A new Main Stand was opened by Sports Minister Denis Howell in December 1968.

Although the club spent £50,000 on safety measures, the Kop and parts of the Main Stand were closed in 1985 because of a lack of access points.

Problems mounted and before the arrival of the new owner in 1987 Tranmere were facing liquidation and a planning application looked like turning Prenton Park into a site for a supermarket. Now, despite Johnson's departure to Everton, it is the pride of the Wirral.

Walsall

The Bescot Stadium has been home to Walsall since 1990. Sir Stanley Matthews opened the £4.5 million ground for a friendly against Aston Villa on 18 August and the first competitive fixture was against Torquay a week later. It was not built all-seater because the club felt fans still preferred to stand, but its design meant future seating was an easy option.

There are seats for 2,323 in the Highgate Stand, 2,115 in the H. L. Fellows Stand and 1,996 in the William Sharp Stand. The only terracing is in the Gilbert Alsop Stand (2,800). The directors' box (seating 70), the executive section (129) and the 13 executive boxes are situated in the H. L. Fellows Stand. Less than a year after it was opened the Bescot Stadium played host to an England v Switzerland B International, a tie which set the stadium attendance record.

Fellows Park was first used by Walsall in 1896 and, apart from a short spell at their previous ground in West Bromwich Road, it remained their home until 1990. It was the scene of the club's famous FA Cup victory over Arsenal in 1933 and at its demise as a sports ground Fellows Park comprised a Main Stand, a covered home end, a half-covered Popular Side and a small section of open terracing for the away fans.

CAPACITY:

9,485

HIGHEST ATTENDANCE:

25,453 v Newcastle Utd,
29 August 1961,
Division Two (Fellows Park);
10,628, England v Switzerland
B International,
20 May 1991 (Bescot Stadium)

CAPACITY 1971:

24,100 (Fellows Park)

Top: Fellows Park in 1947, with the Main Stand to right, and (Middle) in 1978, looking towards the Hillary Street End.

Above: The impressive new Bescot Stadium, with the Highgate Stand nearest camera and terraced Gilbert Alsop Stand to the right.

Watford

Watford spent the first 23 years of their existence at Cassio Road. Vicarage Road was already used as a recreation ground and Watford moved there in 1922, two years after joining the Football League as original members of the new Division Three. One stand was transported from Cassio Road and erected on the west side of the ground and a new 3,500-seater East Stand was built. Concrete terracing and a new West Stand, the Shrodells Stand, arrived just before the war.

Watford's climb from the Fourth to the First Division in the 1970s brought rapid change to Vicarage Road.

New terracing and safety work costing £750,000 was carried out in the late 1970s, the West Stand paddock seated in 1979 and extra seats added to the side of the East Stand in 1982.

CAPACITY:

23,000

HIGHEST ATTENDANCE:

34,099 v Manchester Utd, 3February 1969 FA Cup 4th Round

CAPACITY 1971:

36,000

Faced by demands for a modern stadium, and later by the Taylor Report's all-seater deadline, Watford were not the only club to turn to the Lobb Partnership, architects specialising in sporting facilities. The design drawn up for Vicarage Road made provision for a 20,000-plus all-seater stadium.

The first phase, with seating initially only in the upper tier, was the erection of the Sir Stanley Rous Stand in the summer of 1986. With its distinctive translucent cover and 34 executive boxes, the stand was built on the west side of the stadium to replace the Shrodells Stand. It was officially opened by the club's then chairman, Elton

John, on 18 October 1986. The next stage came in the summer of 1993 when the Vicarage Road terraces were pulled down and a new all-seater North Stand erected and seating added to the lower tier of the West Stand. The Rookery End terraces were demolished in 1994 to make way for a new all-seater South Stand.

Top: Vicarage Road in the 1990s with the impressive Sir Stanley Rous Stand to the left and the all-seater North Stand, erected in the summer of 1993.

Above: Goalmouth action in 1971, two years after the pictured extension to the East Stand was built.

West Bromwich Albion

CAPACITY:

25,118

HIGHEST ATTENDANCE:

64,815 v Arsenal, 6 March 1937, FA Cup 6th Round

CAPACITY 1971:

50,000

The Hawthorns has been periodically upgraded and changed ever since West Bromwich first moved there at the turn of the century and in that respect 1994 was no different.

The sweeping terrace at the Smethwick Road End (away end) was demolished in January 1994 to make way for a new single-tier 6,366 all-seater stand, to be ready for the start of the new season. The standing terrace and lounge at the Birmingham Road End of the ground was demolished in April 1994 to clear the way for a single-tier 8,400 all-seater stand, plus five executive boxes. The cost of the redevelopment, which included new first aid areas and disabled spaces, was £4.2 million. The club have also

declared their intention to redevelop the Rainbow Stand, which would include the introduction of commercial activities on the site.

The Hawthorns has been the home of West Brom since 1900, their first visitors being Derby on 3 September. The small stand on the Handsworth Side, which had been transported from the club's previous ground at Stoney Lane, lasted just four years before it was burnt down. The Main Stand (Halfords Lane) with wooden terracing at the front and seating for 5,000 was improved as Albion enjoyed success; first with promotion to the First Division in 1911 and then an FA Cup Final appearance one year later against Barnsley.

In 1922 the ground hosted its first international when England beat Ireland 2-0. Two years later, in only the second visit of foreign opposition for an international (the first was at Highbury), Belgium went down 4-0.

The Hawthorns ultimately fell out of big-match favour under fierce competition from other grounds, not least nearby Villa Park and Molineux. Changes and upgrades continued nevertheless.

A new corner stand linked the Main Stand with the Smethwick End in 1934, the Main Stand gained a new roof in 1939 and in the late 1940s more seating was added. Another corner stand, this time linking the Main Stand with the Birmingham Road End, went up in 1958 and six years later an all-seater East Stand replaced terracing on the Handsworth Side. This was later renamed the Rainbow Stand when multi-coloured seats were added and executive boxes installed. The Main Stand was rebuilt in the 1980s (including boxes) and a further roofing improvement made at the Smethwick End/Halford Lane corner and at the Birmingham Road End.

Opposite top: A 1947 view across the Hawthorns towards the Birmingham Road End terrace and the Handsworth Side.

Opposite bottom: The Main Stand and Birmingham Road End seen in 1971.

Top: The Main Stand as it appeared in 1992 complete with executive boxes. Contrast this with the same stand in 1970 (Above).

West Ham United

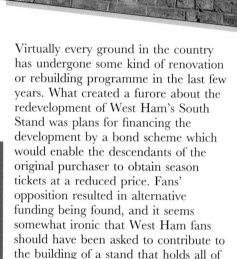

Virtually every ground in the country has undergone some kind of renovation or rebuilding programme in the last few years. What created a furore about the redevelopment of West Ham's South Stand was plans for financing the development by a bond scheme which would enable the descendants of the original purchaser to obtain season tickets at a reduced price. Fans' opposition resulted in alternative funding being found, and it seems somewhat ironic that West Ham fans should have been asked to contribute to the building of a stand that holds all of the visiting supporters in its lower tier.

Known almost universally as Upton Park, West Ham's ground is actually called the Boleyn Ground, named after

CAPACITY:

29,000

HIGHEST ATTENDANCE:

42,322 v Tottenham Hotspur,
17 October 1970,
Division One

CAPACITY 1971:

42,000

a house which stood alongside the ground until the 1950s. West Ham arrived there in 1904 and built a small grandstand on the West Side, a covered bank on the opposite side, a directors' box in one corner and dressing rooms in another. The grandstand was rebuilt complete with dressing rooms in 1913 as the West Stand, and this was much the sight that awaited visitors when the club was admitted to the Football League in 1919.

Success on the field, culminating in an FA Cup Final appearance (the first Wembley final) and promotion in the same year, gave the club the funds to build yet another West Stand, with terracing in front, in 1925. Nothing was allowed to go to waste — the roof from the old West Stand was transferred

across the pitch and provided cover for the South Bank. The east side retained its corrugated iron and timber structure and was known for years as the Chicken Run (the name survived significantly longer than the structure!).

The immediate postwar years were largely spent repairing bomb damage suffered during the Blitz, and it was not until the 1960s that the Boleyn Ground underwent its next phase of redevelopment. A roof was built over the North Bank in 1961, an extra block added to the West Stand in 1965 and the infamous Chicken Run pulled down in 1968 and a new East Stand put up in its place. Although the top tier of this new structure is all-seating, the lower tier still retained terracing and became the new Chicken Run.

Aside from the introduction of seats into the lower tier of the West Stand, the Boleyn Ground remained much the same for the next 20 years or so. After Hillsborough, the cantilevered South Stand was the subject of considerable debate and argument even before work began; with the death of West Ham's favourite son Bobby Moore it was named in his honour and officially opened in March 1994 with a match against a Premier League XI.

There seems little doubt that a similar structure will find its way on to the North Bank, where the crowd are currently so close to the pitch that the players can hear every word uttered. But the Boleyn Ground crowd are for the most part a fair-minded bunch who enjoy their football and expect it to be played a certain way. That way was Bobby Moore's way, and it is fitting that his name will live on at the ground for evermore.

Opposite left: The name plate of a British Rail locomotive once named after the club is now mounted at the ground.

Opposite right: Upton Park as seen in 1965, with the West Stand still awaiting its extra section and the Chicken Run nearest camera.

Below: The Ground in the early 1990s before the building of the Bobby Moore Stand.

Below inset: Looking north across the ground in 1978.

Wimbledon

CAPACITY:

17,619

HIGHEST ATTENDANCE:

30,115 v Manchester Utd,
9 May 1993, FA Premier League
(Selhurst Park);
18,000 v HMS Victory,
1934-35,
FA Amateur Cup 3rd Round
(Plough Lane)

CAPACITY 1971:

18,000 (Plough Lane)

Nobody would accuse Wimbledon of being conformist, so it should have been no surprise that, against all current thinking among other clubs, they struck a groundshare deal with Crystal Palace when they left Plough Lane in 1991. Despite the plea from Justice Taylor for clubs to share grounds, only a handful have taken up the suggestion — and that usually only as a last resort. In that respect at least Wimbledon have similarities with others and for a club that has built its reputation largely on pride it is no surprise that they are still seeking a home of their own.

Until a new ground has been found Wimbledon can console themselves in the facilities of Selhurst Park — certainly a palace after the largely underdeveloped Plough Lane. Ironically the ground which had served the club since 1912 ultimately suffered because of the amazing on-field rise of Wimbledon FC. The climb from non-League to the First Division and FA Cup winners in just 10 years (Wimbledon were elected to the Football League in 1977) is unlikely to be repeated and, although money was spent on improvements, Plough Lane paid for that success.

Plans for a new £17 million stadium at Beddington were reported but after an audacious bid to use Twickenham

(turned down by the Rugby Football Union in February 1991) and unsuccessful talks on sharing Loftus Road, Wimbledon agreed a groundshare deal with Crystal Palace. Ironically, their first scheduled game at Selhurst Park had to be called off because summer work at the ground had not been finished in time.

Top: The homely confines of Plough Lane saw Wimbledon rise from Southern League obscurity to Football League notoriety.

Above: Wimbledon's tenancy at Selhurst Park has frequently seen empty terraces, as are evident in this 1993 view.

Wolverhampton Wanderers

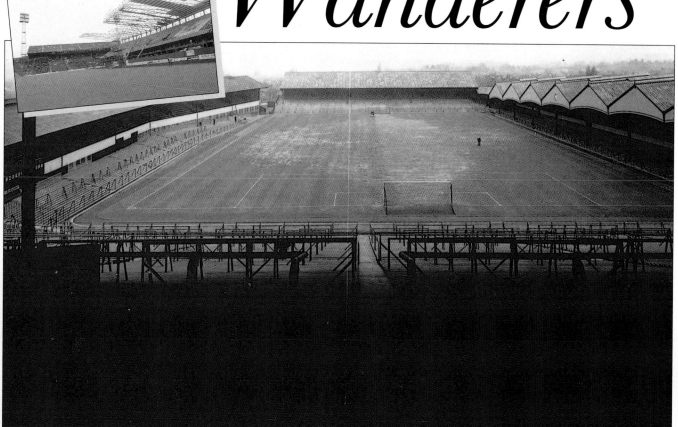

CAPACITY:

28,500

HIGHEST ATTENDANCE:

**61,315 v Liverpool,
11 February 1939,
FA Cup 5th Round**

CAPACITY 1971:

53,500

*The old and the new: Molineux in 1939
(Above) with the Waterloo Road Stand to left,
and its replacement under construction in 1993
(Top). When opened, this was named the
Billy Wright Stand in honour of Wolves' most
celebrated player.*

In the last two decades, perhaps only the development undertaken by Rangers at Ibrox Stadium matches the transformation at Molineux. If the arrival of the 1990s saw Molineux as one superb stand and three dilapidated sides in urgent need of attention, then barely four years later Wolverhampton Wanderers are residents of a ground that would grace the Premier Division.

Before Wolves brought professional football to Molineux the site was known locally for its pleasure gardens, boating lake and a cycle and athletics track. Indeed, the first professional sport at Molineux was cycling. The whole area was watched over from the Molineux Hotel, where the League held many committee meetings in the 1890s. With the help of the Northampton Brewery Company, Wolves built dressing rooms, an office, a small stand which could accommodate 300 and developed some cinder banking and shelter for a further 4,000. Molineux opened its doors for football for the first time in 1889 — Aston Villa were the visitors.

In 1923 the club formed a new limited company which bought the site from the brewery for £5,607 and two years later built their first major stand, with the Waterloo Road Side providing seats for 2,600 and standing room for 4,000. As the club continued its rise back up the League (they returned to the First Division in 1932) so work

continued around the ground. After an old cover had blown down in a gale, a new Molineux Street Stand went up in its place, accommodating 3,400 seats and 4,500 standing places.

This stand is perhaps one of the longest-lived memories of Molineux, for its multi-span roof, tapering towards one end to follow the street, was as distinctive a sight as the Spion Kop at Anfield. Only four other clubs had a similar structure, including Arsenal (in 1913) and Manchester United (in 1909), all now sadly gone. In the years leading up to World War 2 Molineux saw the development of the two ends, with roofs being placed over both the North and South Banks, and remained virtually untouched or unaltered for 30 years or so after the war.

The introduction of the Safety of Sports Grounds Act caused many clubs to re-evaluate their grounds and Wolves, realising that the now all-seater Molineux Street Stand would not pass, decided in 1978 to erect a modern stand in its place. The design, since copied at many Premiership clubs, was revolutionary and extremely impressive then; a curved cantilever stand with two tiers of seating separated only by a tier of private executive boxes. The stand, which contained 9,500 seats and 42 boxes, cost Wolves £2.8 million, but the building of the stand almost finished the club off for good, liquidation in 1982 being staved off thanks to a consortium led by ex-player Derek Dougan. It proved to be something of a false dawn, for four years later the club was back in debt to the tune of £1.8 million and languishing in the Fourth Division: had the club wanted to develop the three other sides of the ground they were in no position to do so. And so the Waterloo Road Stand and North Bank were closed, with only the offices in the former stand remaining open.

In 1986 the South Bank was closed and only the new stand remained open, providing an atmosphere made even more eerie by the distance between the John Ireland Stand (as the stand was christened) and pitch. The stand is so far away from the playing area since Wolves had once planned to rotate the pitch by 90 degrees, making the previous North and South Bank ends into sides. There again, an average gate of 4,016 in 1985-86 could easily be accommodated in the stand.

Now, thanks to wealthy benefactor Sir Jack Hayward and £25 million, Molineux has four stands any supporter can be proud of, creating an atmosphere that once again strikes fear into visiting players. The Wolves logo is picked out in black seats among a forest of old gold ones, giving a striking appearance when the ground is empty. With a Premier-standard ground, Hayward and Wolves are now aiming for a return to the top flight.

Wolves' impressive new Molineux Stadium as seen from pitch level (Above) and from the air (Right).

Inset opposite top: The new North Stand.

Inset opposite bottom: Wolves entertain Chelsea in 1975 with the golden gables of the Molineux Street Stand behind them.

Wrexham

Wrexham's place in Welsh football history is assured. They are the oldest club in Wales and the town is the birthplace of the Welsh FA. Acton Park, Wrexham's original ground, staged Wales' first home international in 1877 (a 2-0 defeat at the hands of Scotland).

Wrexham settled at the Racecourse in 1905, although they had used the ground a few times previously. Some development was carried out in the 1920s and 1930s but concrete terracing was not laid until after World War 2. A tiny 1,000-seat stand, bought from a cinema and dubbed the Pigeon Loft, was erected at the Town End in 1962 and ten years later the Yale Stand was completed. The Border Stand opened in 1978 and the Kop was covered in 1980.

The Racecourse Ground has hosted numerous international fixtures, although there is one record it would prefer to lose. On 27 May 1982, only 2,315 turned up when Wales played Northern Ireland, the lowest attendance for a full Home International this century.

Proposals for the complete redevelopment of the Racecourse Ground, co-ordinated by Freshfields of Chester, are planned to give Wrexham a leading role in Wales' football future as well as its past. The design includes a 15,000-capacity all-seater stadium, plus a hotel, offices, conference halls, cinemas, banks, restaurants and other sporting facilities and parking for 1,500 cars.

CAPACITY:
11,957

HIGHEST ATTENDANCE:
34,445 v Manchester Utd, 26 January 1957, FA Cup 4th Round

CAPACITY 1971:
36,000

Above: Wrexham's Racecourse Ground from the air in 1976, with the old Pigeon Loft clearly evident on the Kop Town End.

Left: This 1993 view shows the covered terracing that replaced it to the right, together with the Yale Stand.

RACECOURSE GROUND

Wycombe Wanderers

CAPACITY:

10,000

HIGHEST ATTENDANCE:

**7,802 v Norwich City,
8 January 1994,
FA Cup Third Round**

cantilevered stands on all four sides; the Main Stand, the *Bucks Free Press* Stand, the Hillbottom Terrace and the Davenport Vernon Stand which accommodates the visiting supporters. Success off the field was reflected by success on it: a 'double' of FA Challenge Trophy and Vauxhall Conference Championship ensuring their elevation to League status, and promotion to the Second Division via the play-offs in their first League season.

While the ground has a comparatively modest capacity of 10,000 (this was raised from 8,000 in the 1994 close season with the addition of further barriers), of which 1,282 are seated, it is exactly the right size for the level of football Wycombe are currently playing. More importantly, securing sponsorship to build new stands and stadia could well be a regular occurrence in the next century. Whatever else they may achieve, Wycombe Wanderers are already trailblazers on that particular score.

Above left: Despite their status as the League's newest club, Wycombe Wanderers have set the pace with their custom-built Adams Park ground. Its current capacity of 10,000 is likely to prove adequate on most occasions, even though they started the 1994-95 season in the Second Division.

It is somehow fitting that Wycombe, the club that in 1993 became the Football League's newest recruit, should be ensconced in what was then the newest stadium; a modern structure that puts many of the grounds in the higher echelons to shame.

When property developers made an offer of £3.5 million for the Loakes Park site where the club had played for 100 years, Wanderers found an alternative site at Hillbottom Road and drew up plans for a custom-built ground costing £3.75 million. The additional money needed for Adams Park came not from grants but by sponsorship from local businesses.

Opened in 1990, the ground features

PAberdeen

CAPACITY:

21,634

HIGHEST ATTENDANCE:

45,061 v Hearts,
13 March 1954,
Scottish Cup 4th Round

CAPACITY 1971:

45,000

In 1978, when seats were installed in the South Stand, Pittodrie became the first all-seater stadium in Britain. It was a move ahead of its time, pre-dating Coventry, the first English club to experiment with an all-seater ground, by three years.

Success, not least in Europe, helped ensure that Aberdeen prospered from the bold experiment. In 1980 several rows of seats in the South Stand were removed when an £800,000 cantilever roof was erected, thus ending discomfort for the fans who had braved the Grampians' weather conditions on uncovered bench seats for the early months of the all-seater move. The following year Aberdeen reaffirmed their faith in their all-seater status by replacing the benches with individual seats. Executive boxes were built at the back of the Main Stand in 1983 and by 1988 the Merkland Stand had been re-roofed and re-seated at a cost of £700,000. In 1993 the £4.5 million Richard Donald Stand was unveiled.

When Dumbarton became the first visitors to Pittodrie on 2 September 1899 facilities included a stand on the north and terraced banking on the east of the ground. Six months later the Granite City watched Scotland beat Wales 5-2 when the ground hosted its first international. (More recently, Pittodrie has been the venue for a friendly against Egypt in 1990 and the World Cup qualifier against Estonia in 1993.)

Pittodrie was, not surprisingly, chosen as the headquarters when, in 1903, the original Aberdeen amalgamated with the town's other two clubs, Victoria United and Orion. The latter brought with them their grandstand (it had to be replaced two years later) and a crowd of 8,000 saw the new Aberdeen draw 1-1 with Stenhousemuir. The club gained election to the Scottish Second Division

at the end of the season and within a year was in the First. Pittodrie has hosted top-flight football ever since.

The interwar years brought real change to Pittodrie with an extension to the south terracing in 1924, a new Main Stand a year later, a cover for the King Street End in 1934 and a small stand at the Beach End three years later. It was also during this time that trainer Donald Colman's desire to keep

his notes dry prompted the building of football's first ever 'dugout'.

The Beach End was covered in 1958 and seven years later the roof on the King Street End was extended. Moves towards making Pittodrie all-seater can be traced to 1968 when seating was added to the enclosure in the Main Stand. This stand and the offices it housed was damaged by a fire in 1971.

Opposite: This view of Pittodrie, taken in 1962, four years after the Beach End was covered, shows the ground's proximity to the North Sea that gave the terrace its name.

Above: Aberdeen's stadium in early 1978. When seats were added to the South Stand later that year, Pittodrie became Britain's first all-seater stadium.

Left: This 1994 picture shows the recently completed £4.5 million Richard Donald Stand which was built at the Beach End.

Dundee

Dens Park and Tannadice are the closest grounds in the whole of Britain; perhaps only in Italy, where a host of clubs share the same ground, are there any two clubs closer.

Dundee were formed in 1893 after the amalgamation of two local clubs, Our Boys and East End, and took up residence at the former's West Craigie Park, although the latter's Carolina Port was undoubtedly the better ground. In time, Dundee realised their mistake and spent five years at Carolina Port, moving to Dens Park in 1898. They brought with them the stand from Carolina Port, placed it on the Dens Road side and built a new Main Stand on Tannadice Street.

Financially secure enough to buy the plot outright in 1919, Dundee began developing the ground in much the same shape that is retained today with the aid of Archibald Leitch — a bowl-shaped ground with extensive terracing around three sides and one main stand that provided the only cover. The new Dens Park was opened in 1921 and was undoubtedly the finest ground in the city, good enough to stage an international between Scotland and Wales in 1936.

Cover was finally provided for the south side terrace after a number of transfers brought in sufficient funds in 1959 but it took until the following decade for the West End Terrace to be similarly covered. In 1975 seating was

added to both the South and West Terraces. While the capacity and revenue is decidedly down on 20 years or so ago, Dundee are keen to exploit their ground to its full potential and have added a greyhound racing track around the football pitch, an action which necessitated the closing of one end while kennels were built!

CAPACITY:

16,871

HIGHEST ATTENDANCE:

**43,024 v Rangers,
7 February 1953,
Scottish Cup 2nd Round**

CAPACITY 1971:

45,000

Above: This early-1960s aerial photograph shows the proximity of Dundee's two football grounds.

Left: Dens Park as viewed from the air in 1994.

Opposite left: Tannadice, home of Dundee United, in 1966.

Opposite right: Opened in 1992, United's North Stand was named the George Fox Stand.

Dundee United

For many years, Dundee United's Tannadice Park saw little change, but success on the pitch during the 1980s, including reaching the UEFA Cup Final, gave the club both the confidence and resources to embark on an almost wholesale change of the ground which bore fruit in the 1990s.

Dundee United began life as Dundee Hibernian and considered using Carolina Port as their first ground before settling on Clepington Park, briefly sharing with East End and Johnstone Wanderers. They enclosed the area soon after their arrival, erected a two-storey Pavilion and built up the banking to accommodate 15,000 spectators. The ground was renamed Tannadice Park and was formally opened with a match against the other Hibernian, those from Edinburgh, before a crowd of 7,000 on 18 August 1909.

The following year the club were admitted to the Scottish Second Division but lost their League status in 1922 and were on the brink of going

bankrupt when a consortium rescued the club, changed the name to Dundee United and returned them to the League, this time the First Division, in 1925.

With new status came new responsibilities and the club bought the ground for £2,500 and then laid terracing around three of the sides which increased capacity to some 30,000. Thereafter Tannadice Park changed little for the next 30 years or so (although the Pavilion was improved in 1931) until a cover was put over the Dens Park End and the Arklay Street End was concreted in 1957. The Pavilion survived for four more years until being hauled down in 1961.

Dundee United then embarked on a considerable amount of construction at Tannadice Park — a new stand was built to replace the Pavilion, the North Terracing was enlarged and the club also built an L-shaped cantilever in one corner of the ground. The capacity of the ground then stood at around 28,500.

CAPACITY:

16,868

HIGHEST ATTENDANCE:

**28,000 v Barcelona,
16 November 1966,
Fairs Cup 2nd Round**

CAPACITY 1971:

28,500

A new North Stand was opened in 1992, a two-tier cantilever stand with accommodation for 5,100 spectators. A new East Stand of much the same design with room for 2,900 was built in 1994. Essential work to bring the West Terracing in line with all-seater stadia was also under way, and that will hold 2,500, leaving just one area of the ground to complete. When finished, Tannadice Park will hold roughly 13,000 spectators. Their near neighbours can at present cast no more than envious glances.

Glasgow Celtic

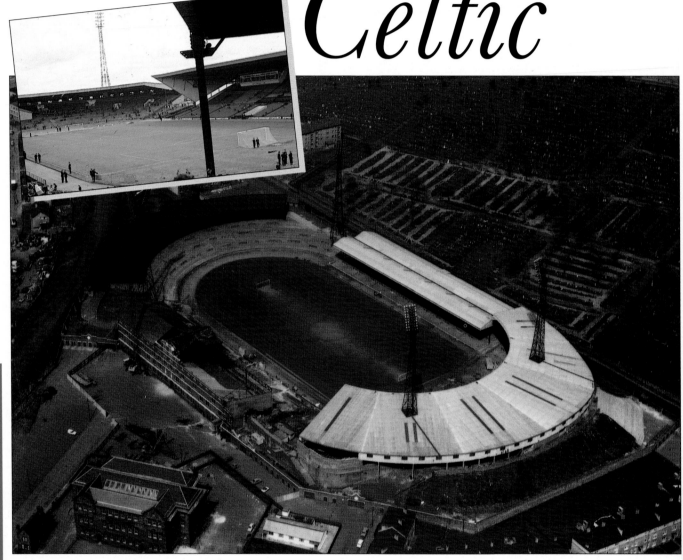

CAPACITY:

34,000

HIGHEST ATTENDANCE:

**92,000 v Rangers,
1 January 1938,
Division One**

CAPACITY 1971:

80,000

As with Rangers and Ibrox Park, Celtic have been playing at Celtic Park since their formation in 1887, although the ground was not officially opened until the following year. Just like their city rivals, Celtic also moved grounds but retained the name, although the circumstances were different; their landlord put the rent up to £450 and so Celtic looked for somewhere else to play. They didn't have far to look: the current Celtic Park (also known as

Parkhead) is barely 200yd from the old.

After an initial period of leasing, Celtic bought the property outright in 1897 for £10,000, although constructing a ground that lived up to the nickname of 'Paradise' had begun in earnest in 1892. At the turn of the century, Celtic Park was already one of the three major venues in Scotland, having stolen a march on its rivals by staging the World Cycling Championships in 1897 and being the

Opposite top: Celtic's South Stand (with suspended press box) and East Terrace.

Opposite: The view in April 1971, as Celtic prepared to give the South Stand (to left of picture) a new roof.

Left: Seen from a similar angle in 1994, eight years after the West End (furthest from camera) was re-roofed.

Below left: The entrance to the South Stand.

Archibald Leitch, although smaller than the new stand at Ibrox which opened the same year. Thereafter development at Celtic Park was at a considerably slower pace than its chief rival, although the Celtic supporters were under cover well before their rivals. The north end terracing was first covered in 1904 and the roof replaced in 1966; the East Terrace was covered in 1957 and following European success in 1968 replaced with an up-to-date design.

The final piece in the Celtic Park jigsaw came in 1971 with the construction of a new canopy style roof over the South Stand, at the same time as converting the stand to an all-seater for 8,686 spectators. A total of £1.5 million was spent in 1991-92 to replace timber flooring and wooden seats.

One of the major problems with Celtic Park is the surprisingly low number of seats among the 1993-94 capacity of nearly 50,000. This fell quite dramatically as the ground was brought in line with new legislation (the north enclosure was first to be seated), but the new consortium which took over the club in 1994 pledged to look at developing a new site and creating a third Celtic Park. If this is not possible, the current site — like Ibrox before it — offers a great many possibilities.

first ground to try fixed floodlights with a match against Clyde in 1893.

Celtic could also claim to have been the first club to try executive boxes — certainly a forerunner of these was built in the Grant Stand, constructed in 1898 and which featured padded seats and sliding windows at the front and sides. The venture was not particularly successful, but it took until 1929 for the Grant Stand to be hauled down and it lasted that long only because of a major fire in the Pavilion and Main Stand on the opposite side in 1904.

A new South Stand was constructed on the Grant Stand's site designed in part by, or certainly in the style of

Glasgow Rangers

CAPACITY:

47,000

HIGHEST ATTENDANCE:

**118,567 v Celtic,
2 January 1939,
Division One**

CAPACITY 1971:

100,000

No other football ground in the British Isles has changed as dramatically as Ibrox Park in the last 20 years, and few grounds have such a history of mixed fortunes.

Although Rangers have played at Ibrox since 1887, it was a different Ibrox then; the first was situated next door to the current stadium and was inaugurated with a match against Preston in August 1887. It was the success Celtic had enjoyed in being given internationals to stage that

Top: The main entrance to Ibrox, pictured during the 1970-71 season.

Above right: Ibrox Park from the air in 1947, with Archibald Leitch's famous South Stand visible nearest the camera.

Opposite top: The South Stand remains – but everything else is new in the 1990s.

Opposite below: The two-tier Govan Stand which faces the South Stand.

Inset bottom: The daunting gates of Ibrox.

prompted Rangers move to a bigger site in 1899, even though the first Ibrox was a regular venue for the Scottish Cup Final during the 1890s.

Some of the building work was of a decidedly temporary nature, none more so than the wooden terracing built at the West End on a tall iron and wood framework. The first time it was tested to its capacity it was found sadly

wanting: the Scotland v England match on 5 April 1902 saw the worst football disaster for the next 40 years, with 26 people falling some 50ft to their deaths when the structure gave way as the crowd strained for a better view of the football action. A further 500 were injured.

Rangers set about rebuilding Ibrox, this time with more solid materials.

Archibald Leitch was brought in to supervise, and he made the club use solid earth banking for the terracing rather than wood. Ibrox's capacity slid from 68,000 at the turn of the century (some 75,000 were in attendance at the disaster match) to a mere 25,000 by 1905. Leitch continued his work for the next 20 years or so; the ground, a giant oval-shaped arena with a covered stand along one length and three open sides of terracing, could hold 63,000 by 1910.

Success on and off the field (Ibrox gradually took over from Celtic as a viable alternative to Hampden Park and also held other sporting events, such as athletics and cycling) saw the construction of Leitch's most memorable stand in 1928. Similar in design to but grander in size than stands at Roker, Goodison and Fratton Park, the South Stand was a 10,000-seater with a magnificent castellated press box on its roof.

The rest of the ground continued upwards and outwards, so by 1939 Ibrox was able to hold a British record crowd figure for a League match, when 118,567 crowded in for the traditional New Year match against Celtic. Only Hampden in Britain was bigger. And once the ground had gone as high and as far out as it could, Rangers put on roofs to keep some of the thousands dry.

The worst football disaster in Britain bar Hillsborough in 1989 occurred at Ibrox on 2 January 1971. Thousands of Rangers fans were streaming out of the ground, many on Stairway 13, when a goal was scored and some fans tried to climb back: a number of steel barriers gave way and 66 people died.

Although there were minor alterations over the next two years as a consequence, radical plans were already being drawn up which would transform Ibrox. Rangers, Britain's richest football club, justified the tag by spending somewhere in the region of £10 million on building three new stands at a time when Wolves were contemplating bankruptcy after spending £2 million on just one.

Archibald Leitch's South Stand was retained, a vital and romantic link with Rangers' past, but had 7,300 seats added on top, including corporate hospitality facilities. The oval shape went out and in its place came three identical stands that incorporated office space and an exhibition suite. In 1994, the final standing enclosures in front of the oldest stand were seated, losing 1,500 from the overall capacity which declined to 47,000 — of which 33,000 were occupied by season ticket holders — though a similar number of seats had been added in 1993 by the expedient of dropping the pitch 10in.

Though the Ibrox that resulted remains no less a daunting place for away teams, it is now an altogether safer place for visiting and home supporters.

Heart of Midlothian

In light of the cramped circumstances at Tynecastle it is surprising to learn that the club propose virtually rebuilding the ground from scratch rather than consider moving to a new venue as local rivals Hibernian intend. Perhaps the club with the most romantic name in British football couldn't bear to end this century in much the same way they ended the last!

Hearts took up residence at Tynecastle in 1881, then located where Wardlaw Street and Wardlaw Place now stand. This became their home for the next five years until a move to Gorgie Street, although in keeping with many Scottish clubs, Hearts retained the name of the ground for their new venue. The final match at the Old Tynecastle took place in February 1886.

Facilities at the new ground were hardly palatial: a modest Pavilion and stand were completed in 1903 and work on the Main Stand did not commence until 1914, even though the club had already won two League Championships and four Scottish Cups. The club bought the property outright in 1926 and expanded the terracing until a capacity of over 50,000 was

CAPACITY:

25,177

HIGHEST ATTENDANCE:

53,496 v Rangers,
13 February 1932,
Scottish Cup 3rd Round

CAPACITY 1971:

49,000

possible. However, Tynecastle was already proving to be somewhat limiting and the club gave serious thought to moving to a new venue, with both Murrayfield and Sighthill being strongly considered. In the end they stayed put.

The ground itself is virtually hidden by the surrounding buildings, although the occupants of one tenement have a cosy view of the proceedings from the Gorgie Road End — the first executive boxes? While the entrance to the Main Stand has been suitably modernised, the stand itself is as one would expect for its age (80 years old). Opposite lies

the Wheatfield Street side, a former terrace now bedecked with maroon and white bench seating with a covering that goes round the corner to provide some cover for the occupants of the McLeod Street End.

Top: Despite its lack of potential for expansion, as shown in this 1972 aerial view, Tynecastle will remain Hearts' home for the foreseeable future.

Above: The view from pitch level, as seen when Celtic visited in 1985.

Hibernian

CAPACITY:

?1,899

HIGHEST ATTENDANCE:

55,860 v Heart of Midlothian,
? January 1950,
Division One

CAPACITY 1971:

60,000

The call for all-seater stadia as detailed in the Taylor Report has resulted in clubs choosing either to rebuild or renovate their existing stadia, or capitalising on the property value of their grounds and moving to a custom-built stadium elsewhere.

Hibernian intend to move in 1995 from Easter Road, where they have played since 1893, to an out-of-town site where four cantilevered stands will provide accommodation for 15,000 spectators — a project that is likely to cost in the region of £11-£12 million.

The current Easter Road ground is some 40yd from its original position, having been moved in the 1920s so that the club could make the pitch itself level. At the same time a new stand was built on the West Side and the ground opened in 1924 with a capacity of 45,000 spectators. The East Side terracing was developed after World War 2, enabling a record crowd of 65,860 to squeeze into Easter Road, although additional plans to raise each end to a similar height were subsequently shelved.

Although a cover was added to the North Terrace in the early 1960s, Easter Road did not change until 1975 when the Safety of Sports Grounds Act brought bench seating to the North End (it being cheaper to install than new crush barriers). Ten years later the East Side was effectively reduced by half by lowering the height and installing a large cover, the only other subsequent major alteration being the installation of executive boxes below the Main Stand.

If the proposed move is delayed, then the club will be expected to install seating or close the terraced parts of the ground.

The major visible difference between Easter Road in 1972 (Top) and 1994 (Left) is the roof that was added to the East Side – an alteration which significantly reduced the depth of terracing available.

Future Grounds

Artistic impressions of futuristic-looking football grounds are nothing new. Many clubs have had their dreams and aspirations, but in reality they found their current home had to serve their needs. Even ten years ago new football grounds seemed only dreams and artistic impressions remained just that. As supporters of Oxford and Southampton have discovered, hopes of a modern new ground can easily be thwarted by opposition from local people and planners. Football supporters could have been forgiven for thinking that nobody really wanted them to have new stadia.

A small number of forward-thinking clubs have changed all that. Many designs are finally being transformed from the drawing board into steel and concrete. Scunthorpe, Walsall, Chester, Wycombe, Millwall and, most recently, Huddersfield have all moved to new grounds built specifically for their needs. Chester have a neat, uniform, 6,000-capacity stadium, with some terracing. Millwall have a more extensive 20,000 all-seater stadium, built not only for football but also for staging other sporting and musical events. Different needs. Different stadia. All these clubs have proved that what once seemed impossible can come true and have given inspiration and hope to other clubs searching for new grounds.

When it comes to design, safety is the number one priority for any new stadium or stand. A number of safety guidelines are set out in the Green Guide under the 1975 Safety of Sports Grounds Act and general Building Regulations obviously apply. In addition to this the Football Stadia Advisory Council have issued a number of guidance documents covering such

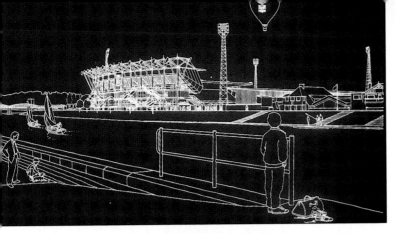

topics as toilets, PA systems, seating, terracing and control rooms, while the FIFA Stadia Criteria offer another guide to good design.

Many clubs have specific requirements regarding safety, such as location of emergency telephones or stewards' seating. One of the most striking examples of exceeding the minimum safety requirements is at the new Kirklees Stadium, Huddersfield, which has an emergency access road — a throughway not used by any traffic other than emergency vehicles — crossing the car park.

The requirement for grounds to be all-seater is clearly the major change as regards safety in recent years, but many other elements are interlinked with this all-important aspect.

Pre-match entertainment can help ensure that spectators arrive in a steady flow and not all a few minutes before the game starts. In itself this can be a major safety measure. But entertainment has moved on from the marching band days. Club rooms, restaurants, television screens showing replays and highlights and more recently the amusement arcade in Highbury's North Stand all contribute to getting people into grounds earlier. The introduction of small, individual television screens (as in airliners) and more widespread use of in-ground radio for news, results and commentary are also predicted for the future.

Top: Lobb Partnership's design for the Trent End at Nottingham Forest Football Club.

Left: If it had been approved, Bristol Rovers' proposed new home as part of the Severnside Sportsworld complex would have been a far cry from their current lodgings at Bath City's Twerton Park.

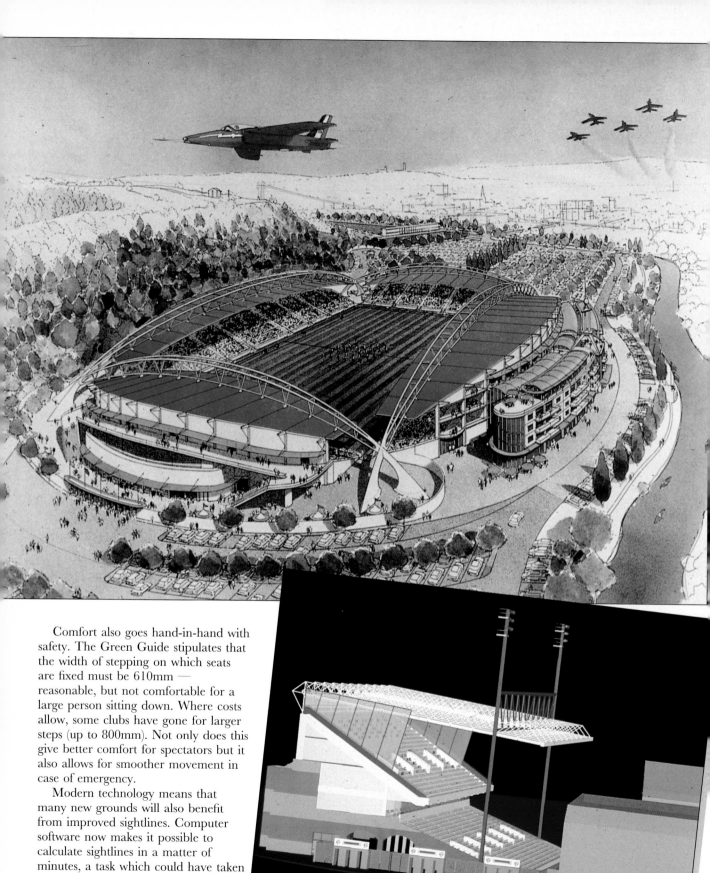

Comfort also goes hand-in-hand with safety. The Green Guide stipulates that the width of stepping on which seats are fixed must be 610mm — reasonable, but not comfortable for a large person sitting down. Where costs allow, some clubs have gone for larger steps (up to 800mm). Not only does this give better comfort for spectators but it also allows for smoother movement in case of emergency.

Modern technology means that many new grounds will also benefit from improved sightlines. Computer software now makes it possible to calculate sightlines in a matter of minutes, a task which could have taken months in the past. Clubs can now predict the 'quality' of the view each

particular stand will provide for each spectator, as carried out for supporters in the new North Bank Stand at Arsenal.

Spectator facilities will also improve as more clubs begin to develop their ground for events other than football. Design of the New Den, for instance, has taken into account Millwall's desire to use the ground for pop concerts and other sporting events. One of the

biggest changes to new grounds will be the increased size of the concourses and a greater number of toilet facilities. Concert promoters require access for the large trucks which supply the stage and lighting equipment. Good quality covering for the pitch during such events is another requirement, and, as at the Kirklees Stadium, generators may be needed to back up the power supply for the large lighting displays.

Opposite top: A future ground that has already become a reality – Huddersfield's Kirklees Stadium.

Opposite bottom: Lobb Partnership's design for Norwich City's Barclay Stand redevelopment.

Top: The proposed development of Middlesbrough's Ayresome Park and (Above) Portsmouth's hoped for new Parkway stadium.

Providing facilities for business is one area no club can ignore. Although despised by some fans, business spectators provide crucial income to many clubs. Conference, seminar and banqueting, as well as matchday facilities are not only money-spinners but they also ensure that the ground is being used throughout the week and not just for a few hours on Saturdays.

Football has for a long time been seen as a male preserve, so it is probably not surprising that clubs have been slow in providing facilities for their female and younger supporters. The successful introduction of baby-changing facilities and crêches at clubs like Brentford, however, has shown that there is a real demand for such provision. Designers of new grounds have taken note; to such an extent that a Women's Action Group was involved in discussions over the development of the Kirklees Stadium. Crêches are usually near to the grounds, so children can be dropped off and collected away from the main throng of spectators.

Above: Although one of the League's most traditional clubs, Burnley hope to turn Turf Moor into a ground fit for the next century.

Right: A design study for a stadium of the 1990s and beyond.

Overleaf: Lobb Partnership's design for developing Birmingham City's St Andrews stadium.

The number of spaces allocated to disabled supporters has increased gradually over the last few years, as have facilities. Building platforms for disabled supporters can improve viewing but there is also the consideration of safety in the case of emergency. On the other hand, while areas on the edge of the pitch are safer, views are poorer. Split-level sites make it possible to design safe and satisfactory viewing areas for the disabled fan, but flatter sites must balance comfort and good viewing with safety.

With so many aspects to balance in the design of our future football stadia (finance is ultimately the controlling factor), some feel the result will be a nation full of cloned, characterless football grounds. Many elements of design will no doubt be repeated, as indeed they have been in the past, but with imagination from architects and clubs alike, each ground — new or old — can capture its own special place in the history of British football.